Lessons from the Past

With best wishes
Anne Watkinson 22.07.19

LESSONS FROM THE PAST

A history of Manor Street School, Braintree

Written and compiled by Anne Watkinson
with the assistance of Diana Nayler
for Braintree District Museum Trust Ltd
Manor Street,
Braintree,
Essex CM7 3HW.
Telephone 01376 325266

First Published 2018

Limited Edition typeset in Garamond 13 pt.

Designed & Published by The Millrind Press

www.millrind.co.uk

ISBN. 978 1902 194 15 8

Printed by,

The Lavenham Press Ltd

Dedication

This book is dedicated to the memories of two of its former pupils who sadly died while it was being compiled. Both were interviewed for their memories during our research. Mike Baker was well known locally for his accounts of Braintree history, but was also a nationally renowned educational journalist. He broadcast and wrote widely, sometimes referring to his old school. Marion Booth not only was a pupil but was also a teacher at the school before and after her marriage. All her three girls came to the school, her husband chaired the PTA and taught cycling proficiency after school. As a Friend of the Museum, she continued her interest until ill health prevented her.

Contents

Foreword

Schools generally are more crucial in our individual and collective lives than is sometimes understood. Their nurturing influence is second only to our families. Their complex reverberations are felt everywhere. Manor Street School stands as exemplar for those realities. That is no accident, for it was founded by a group of local dignitaries, led by the Unitarian businessman George Courtauld, in a spirit of high Victorian idealism, which we could well do with in these times.

When my wife Penelope and I were deciding where to send our trio Caitlin, Alice and Oliver, I remember being struck by those explicitly non sectarian, Christian origins. We sensed, after meeting the then Head, Mr. Tyler, that that flame was still burning brightly. We never had cause to regret sending the children to the school and they and we were grateful for the experience. Names such as Mr. Broad, Mr Butler and Mrs Michaels need little excavation to come to life, caring, committed and skilful as they were.

Thus it is right and good that the life and times of Manor Street School should be permanently celebrated in this publication. In a short termist, overbusy era the quiet, ongoing inspiration of histories such as this are easily lost for ever and that would be sad, as you may judge for yourselves. We owe much to those who have initiated and so well delivered this challenging project, especially Anne, who took over from Mr. Tyler and Diana, the Friends of Braintree District Museum and the Museum Manager, Robert Rose.

I am sure it will generate great pleasure and re-kindle affection for Manor Street School amongst all those connected with it, not least its former governors, teachers and pupils.

Andrew Phillips, Lord Phillips of Sudbury.

Preamble

As the 150th anniversary of the opening of the building approached, it seemed a good time to produce an illustrated account which we hoped would be of interest, not only to visitors to the museum and those associated with the school but also a wider audience. That 150th anniversary year was marked by exhibitions and events to share memories and extended further our understanding of what went on in the school. There was an even greater need to capture the stories of pupils and staff while we could, the school already having been closed for over twenty years. We were able to use modern recording, scanning and printing techniques along with internet research which made it much easier to write and produce such a book.

A short history of the school was written for the 100th anniversary by the then headteacher, Miss Jarvis. This exists as a small pamphlet in the museum archive. The occurrence of the 125th anniversary was marked by a pageant and tea parties and a modest attempt to collect photographs, artefacts and accounts of time spent at the school.

The author and co author both had a personal interest in the school and the area it served. It was Anne's first headship, a bit of a baptism by fire for many reasons. During that time. while still a popular school, proud of its reputation and the standard of education achieved, the closure procedures were operated. She was also there for the 125th celebrations. Diana, Di, also taught in the Braintree area and used the museum as a resource for her work with pupils. Her historical expertise and less direct involvement has brought a more objective perspective to the work. She was also experienced in oral history.

While it has taken some years for the book to be published, the lessons it points up are still relevant today and the memories of value to the community of Braintree. The book may be of wider interest to those concerned with the education of children and young people everywhere.

Many of the archives are in the museum itself ,others are in the Essex Record Office ERO, such as the log books written by the various heads of the school and the managers' minutes. The historical material is supplemented by contemporary reminiscences of people associated with the school in its lifetime. The detailed dates of each ERO volume are given in the list of references at the end of the book.

Lessons from the Past

Acknowledgements

We wish to thank:

The Friends of Braintree District Museum for their continued support of and interest in the project and help at the open morning particularly Jean Harrison, their chairperson for her persistence. She and her husband have helped with proof-reading;

the staff of both the ERO and the Braintree District Museum who were so helpful in giving us access where they could to artefacts, photographs and documents associated with the school. A full list of the sources of those reproduced in the book is at the end of the book;

Essex Community Fund and the Friends of Braintree District Museum, for financial support;

the many people who over the years shared their memories, showed their photographs and artefacts to the pupils and staff while the school was still running as well as at events since and the additional contributions of text;

interviewees in the search for memories. Some married interviewees used their maiden names only so that those who were at Manor Street School might recall them. We have included the dates during which they were at the school;

Derek Hurst and John Kay for their help and advice over technical matters,

and especially John Kay who spent so many hours enhancing the old photographs and without whose help in the graphic design and publishing expertise we would never have been able to get into print.

Contributors

TEACHERS

Marion Booth 1970-1990
Eric Broad 1947-1981
Steve Burnup 1989-1990
Steve Butler 1975-1987
Margaret Deer 1988-1990
Andy Jones 1989-1990
Jenny Rumbelow 1951-1961, 1971-1990

PUPILS

Sheila Ambrose, née Phillipson, 1943-1949
Mike Baker 1961-1965
Marion Booth 1945-1950
Amy Deer 1985-1990
Kevin Dodman 1964-1971
Maureen Gibson 1945-1951
Gordon Gilbert 1947-1952
Christine Hart 1947-1952
Ron Hutley 1926-1934
Robert Lockwood 1931-1937
Gillian Panton 1956-1962
Bryan Panton 1952-1958
Frances Parker 1926-1932
Caitlin Phillips 1975-1981
Claire Rennie 1973-1979
Anne Rolfe, née Gooderham. 1944-1949
Michael Rolfe 1939-1945
Margaret Sweeting 1950-1957
Patricia Thorogood, née Richardson. 1943-1949
Freda Watts, née Earl. 1941-1947

ESSEX COUNTY COUNCIL

Don Parker

WRITTEN CONTRIBUTIONS

were received from:
Sally Amos, née Hart. 1957-1963
Sally Bloomfield 1954-1956
Karen Bowden, née Sizeland. 1977-1983
Ann Cohen 1950-1954
Jean and David Grice
Angela Gridley, née Cooper. 1949-1955
David Kemp 1952-1958
Jemma Longland 1987-1990
Angela Macdonald, née Cornell. 1957-1963
Jackie Millyard, née Leech. 1962-1965
Malcolm Morris 1961-1967
William Pannell 1963-1967
Francis Parker 1926
Andrew Phillips, Foreword.
Robert Rose, Museum Manager.
P.W. Smith 1910-1919
Helen Tate 1972-1979
Bridie Williamson 1986-1990

Memories, photos and contact details are also posted on the Manor Street School Facebook page from time to time

ABBREVIATIONS USED

ERO   Essex Record Office
WW1   World War 1
WW2   World War 2

Chapter 1 Introduction

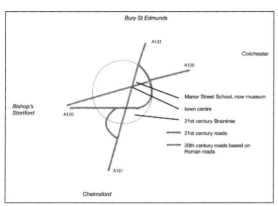

Fig. 1.1 Map showing location of Braintree

The mid nineteenth century was for Braintree, as for many other towns in Great Britain, a time of growing prosperity. From a village 4000 years ago it had grown into a thriving market town, serving the surrounding rural area of north Essex, getting its charter in 1199. It was also a centre of weaving and woollen industries from the fourteenth century.

As these industries were dying out, the Courtauld family settled there and opened a silk mill, as well as mills in Halstead and Bocking. The coming of the railway in 1848 aided the expansion, especially of the arable and livestock market. Along with other philanthropic gestures and buildings, the Courtaulds established

Photo 1.1 The earliest known image of the building 1864.

17

Manor Street School, financing a grand new building and providing an endowment for its running. Many towns have similar industrial heritage and benefactors but Manor was an unusual school. Its history reflects the changes in education and society in Braintree and the wider country over its lifetime.

The 1861 building still exists and in 2012 it was 150 years since it was officially opened. It was an additional building to one already on the site but a new foundation. This 1861 building now houses a thriving, award winning museum. The school to be run in the 1861 building was unusual in having a non sectarian foundation. It was also unusual in being closed in 1990 while still a well loved and successful school. Sadly, this striking building in a central location proved a difficult building to run through most of its life as a school and the site proved limiting for a large school with a broad curriculum.

The original building became the infant school and the main new 1861 building became what was sometimes called the mixed school and later the junior school. There is a list of the various names found for the school at the end of the book. It will be referred to generally in the text as Manor Street School, its familiar name as it was known in the community. Two log books were both started at the same time, when it became a statutory procedure, in 1863. There was one for infants and one for the older children and young people, pupils stayed there until they were 13 or 14 years old until 1938.

A new infant building was erected in 1897 and for a few years at the turn of the century, three buildings were in use. A 1911 extension to the 1861 building finally displaced the old 1850s schoolroom. Two schools, infant and junior, were separately managed until their amalgamation in 1952, when both buildings operated as one school until the closure. A Horsa building, erected on the opposite side of the road was erected after the Second World War, to serve as a canteen, also stayed until closure.

Much of the early history is confusing. This is partly due to the lack of documentary evidence of a time beyond living memory and partly due to the confusing history of education in England. Later in the school's history there are photographic records, first of a very formal nature and later still, verbatim accounts from those who were closely associated with the school.

The National Context

Education at the time of the building of the school was not compulsory nor was it in any way controlled by a local authority or the national government. At the beginning of the nineteenth century only a small proportion of the population received elementary education. Curtis reckoned there was probably less literacy than in Tudor times.[1] Only one sixteenth of children attended school at all. The industrial revolution and the Napoleonic wars had taken their toll. The need was for unskilled labour for the mines and factories. British educational history has often been dominated by political or financial interests rather than educational or social ones. Even today, there is a mixture of funding and control systems and controversy over curricula and pedagogy in contrast to the structuring found in some other countries. The movement of many to towns, the dire poverty in which they lived, the hold that the moneyed classes had on politics and the conflicts between the various Christian denominations all added to the problems.

It was not until the 1833 Factory Act that children under 9 years of age would be prevented from working at all, 9 to 13 year olds allowed to work no more than 48 hours a week and 14 to 18 year olds were restricted to 69 hours a week in all textile factories except those making silk goods. Braintree's early industrial heritage was largely based on the weaving industry in the early nineteenth century. The Courtauld family, which had established the mills in Braintree and Bocking were also philanthropists and it is due to their generosity that Manor Street School was built.

Earlier, charities or private individuals had built and run schools. The charity schools came under two main umbrellas. The Church of England charity schools and their related endowments, were under the auspices of the Society for Promoting Christian Knowledge,

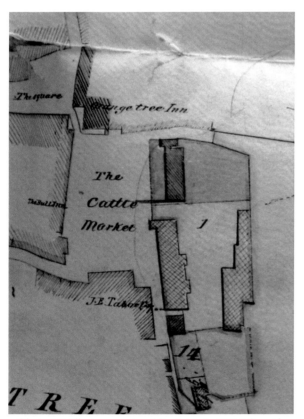

Photo 1.2 The town centre of Braintree in 1844 from the deeds of Hyde Farm.

SPCK. This they called the National Society for promoting the education of the poor in the principles of the established church. These were the National Schools. These schools had a board of management with the incumbent as the chairman. The non-conformist or dissenters' schools had come together under the British and Foreign School Society and known as British Schools. The schools supported by the British Society had an elected committee to run them. Outside of these two main umbrellas were Wesleyan and Roman Catholic schools which had a minister or priest chairing the board.

Attempts at reform foundered. The Church of England opposed undenominational education. Non-conformist churches wanted their particular doctrinal approach promulgated in their schools. The government first proposed that funding to build schools could come from manufacturers and the gentry and the only religious teaching to be scripture study and no worship except the Lord's Prayer. Both the established Church and non-conformists objected. In 1833 the government finally proposed £20,000 for the building of schools for the education of the poorer classes, to be paid when half was raised by public subscription, very like our current matched funding from lottery sources. They gave half to each of the big societies to administer.

Of course, children were not employed on Sundays, nobody was and this encouraged the growth of Sunday Schools. Even with the Sunday Schools, there was a fear that education might spread the kind of sedition that had so disrupted France in the late eighteenth century, although their purpose was largely religious and little of the 3Rs was taught. Spelling was seen as a preparation for reading the Bible. There were a few factory schools, some charity schools and a few dame schools which were little more than overcrowded child-minding establishments.

By 1856, the Committee of Commission, which had been the source of regulations about schools without the ideas going through parliament, became a government education department, with leaders who were appointed by the prime minister of the day. It gives some indication of the priority given to education in the mid nineteenth century when one compares the cost of the Crimean War at 78 million, with the grants for schools. The societies were given £150,000 in 1851 and £541,133 in 1857. Despite this, people were alarmed at the cost of education.

The background to the opening of Manor Street Schools

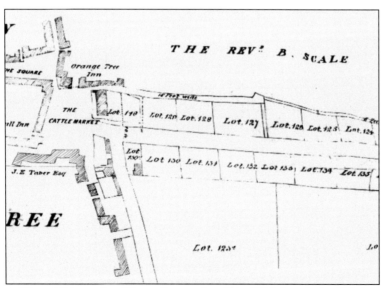

Photo 1.3 Lots along Manor Street to be sold in 1853 from deeds of Hyde Farm.

What organisation there was in towns, was done locally, originally by a committee of Vestry. They would have levied a rate to pay for law and order, water pumps and the Poor Law. In Braintree, this was replaced in 1835 by the Braintree Union with a Board of Guardians. The founding of Manor Street Schools, in the building we know, was part of a movement common in the nineteenth century. Mike

Baker's account of schools in Braintree gives some local details.[2] There had been a Braintree Grammar School for a time. John Ray the botanist attended it but it closed in the seventeenth century. The other schools mentioned were various charity schools dependent on local endowments and the support of the British Society and the National Society. There was a British School in Martin's Yard run by the Vicar and another in Manor Street. Another, Coker's School, closed in 1853 and was also run in accordance with the doctrine and discipline of the Church of England. Bocking End had a Charity School founded by the Bocking Independent Congregation. There were four private schools which served the middle class children, the offspring of farmers and tradesmen. The gentry sent their children to the big national Public Schools. The deeds of the transfers of land, which the museum and the Essex Record Office still hold, are difficult to read, being over a metre wide and written in arcane legal jargon and beautiful but not very legible, copperplate script. Detailed measurements are given of the pieces of land involved in the documents and their siting relative to other pieces of land. There are few maps or plans. One document mentions the ownership of a piece of Manor Farm in 1706, Mark's Manor, as one of three Saxon manors dated from 1086, the Domesday Book. Bardell says this is responsible for the name of Manor Street and thus the schools.[3] Photos 1.2 & 1.3

Deeds of 1844 and 1845 have some maps showing the area around the centre of the town as part of Hyde Farm which was then divided up into lots to be sold off for building.

An 1848 conveyance shows Sir William Foster of Hyde Farm gradually selling off bits of his land. The railway is built through the southern part. The 1849 conveyance shows George Courtauld senior and his brother Samuel, beginning to accumulate different small parcels of land in Manor Street. Eventually these provided a sufficient site for a new building and a playground across the road. Photos 1.4 & 1.5

There is a transfer of land for £52 10s between George Vavasseur and what becomes the group of trustees for the school.

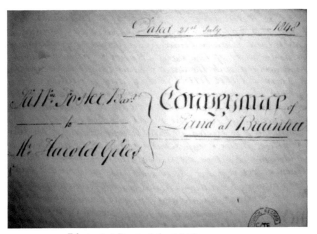

Photo 1.4 Part of the 1848 conveyance.

George Courtauld of Bocking
George Courtauld the younger
Rev. David Rees
James Challis of Lindsell, a farmer
Edward George Craig

George Vavasseur was also a silk manufacturer in the area. The sale was leasehold but for a lease of 500 years, *'for the purpose of requiring that all buildings to be erected on the ground hereafter should front the new road there and*

21

Photo 1.5 Part of the 1849 conveyance.

prohibiting the carrying on of noisome and offensive trades ... breadth of frontage 40 feet and length 90 feet bounded on or towards the west by ground on which a schoolroom has lately been erected.' Another deed continues *'upon trust permit the said premises and all the buildings thereon erected to be appropriated and used as and for a school for the education of children and adults or children of the labouring, manufacturing and other poorer classes and for a residence if so required for the teacher or teachers ... management of a committee to consist of not more than 12 to be annually elected, seven should be chosen by donors of not less than, £5 and annual subscribers of not less than 10s.'* Yet another deed, this time dated 1861, refers to a piece of ground in Manor Street, Braintree, 'on part whereof a building known as Manor Road School has been erected was conveyed and assured to the said ... the trustee group ... upon certain trusts for educational purposes ... certain pieces and parcels of land or ground 'on part of which a building used as an infant school has been erected and built ... specified for educational and literary purposes.'

The foundation of the Manor Street Schools was thus an amalgamation of the new establishment and an existing one run by the then Baptist minister, Dr. Rees. The details of the teachers, governance and the intended recipients of teaching, the poorer classes, appear in many of the deeds for the new main school. Dr. Rees is also empowered by these early deeds to use the building for a Sunday school connected with the Baptist Church.

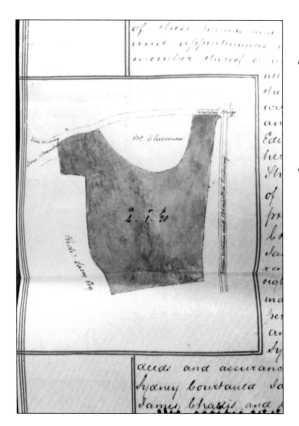

Photo 1.6 Map of site of Chapel Field from 1863

Evening classes could be held there and public lectures. Other pieces of land seemingly on the other side of the road were bought in 1857 and there is a possibly related request in 1857 for a balance of purchase money of £2,657.

George Courtauld also gave £1,000 '*to be invested in good real or government securities to give income for the following purposes:*

repairs, rates and taxes,
keeping the playground and fences in good order and condition,
cleaning, warming and lighting,
keeping in repair the school apparatus or furniture or appointments of said schoolroom, any surplus being used for an extension.'

Another piece of land called Horse Fair on Hither Hyde Field belonging to Braintree Manor Farm was bought in 1866 by Louis Courtauld and later transferred to the school trustees in 1869. Chapel Field was bought in 1863 as part of the endowment investment.

The new building

The original bell, rescued when the steeple was repaired in 1981, is dated 1861 and the writing on the foundation stone, according to the Braintree and Bocking Advertiser of Wednesday, April 9th 1862, read as follows:

'*This school erected and endowed by George Courtauld of Bocking is by him given for the*
use of the children of the poorer classes of this town and neighbourhood.'
Photo 1.7

The foundation stone is now plastered over. Photo 1.8

Photo 1.7 Bell in use in 1980 and the original old bell from the steeple.

A lengthy account of the opening ceremony on Monday April 7th 1862 appears in the following week's paper and forms the basis of the next chapter. It is common with new public buildings, that they become operational and then have an official opening after the

The format of this book

This introduction being chapter 1, chapter 2 describes the opening ceremony and the hopes for the new school. Chapter 3 covers the Victorian era and Chapter 4 takes the story over the turn of the century, when great changes in British and Braintree society were taking place. These chapters depend mainly on references from the log books. These books 'were usually intended to be confidential.' Information to be given was not strictly specified but it was customary to note any untoward events. These would typically include significant levels of absenteeism among children and the causes of this, problems with parents, children and other

Photo 1.8 East gable end of the building showing the site of the original foundation stone under the window, now rendered over

members of staff, social events and fundraising activities, visits to the school by the local gentry, the clergy and others, seasonal activities such as nature walks and gardening, misbehaviour and corporal punishment, which may be entered in a separate punishment book and national events which impinged on school life.' [4]

Chapter 5 covers the period of the First World War and up to the beginning of the Second World War, where we begin to have some real accounts of life in the school. Chapter 6 covers the Second World War and the mid twentieth century. Chapter 7 covers the last years of the school and the reasons

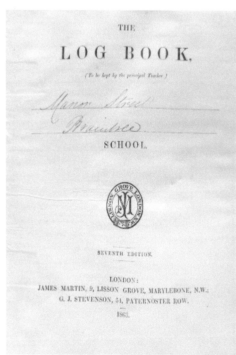

Photo 1.9 Title page of first infant log book.

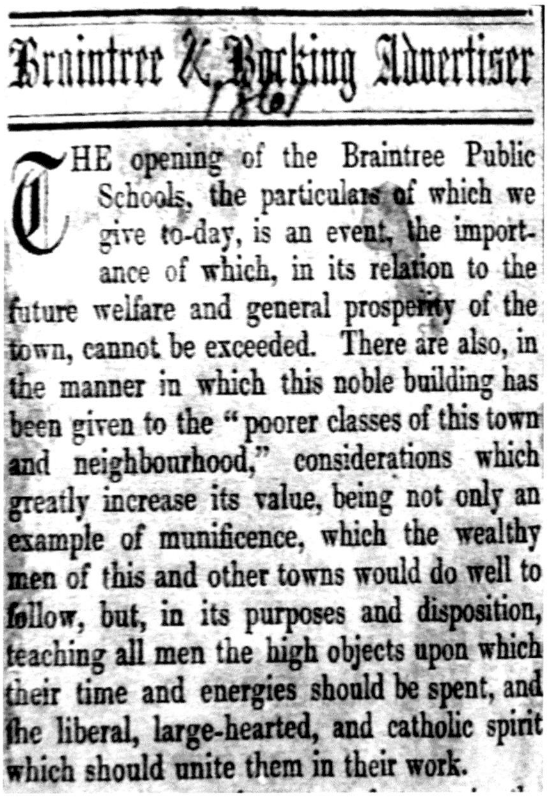

Braintree & Bocking Advertiser

THE opening of the Braintree Public Schools, the particulars of which we give to-day, is an event, the importance of which, in its relation to the future welfare and general prosperity of the town, cannot be exceeded. There are also, in the manner in which this noble building has been given to the "poorer classes of this town and neighbourhood," considerations which greatly increase its value, being not only an example of munificence, which the wealthy men of this and other towns would do well to follow, but, in its purposes and disposition, teaching all men the high objects upon which their time and energies should be spent, and the liberal, large-hearted, and catholic spirit which should unite them in their work.

Photo 1.10 The start of the cutting from the Braintree Advertiser 16 04 62. Added date incorrect

for its closure. The penultimate chapter brings the story up to date. The main chapters are divided into themes giving the historical context, the people and children, the teaching and learning, health issues and notes on the building itself. Things like evidence about special occasions or the impact of war are also dealt with. The final chapter offers some thoughts on the lessons that could be learnt from such a history of a school's life.[4]

The original text quoted verbatim from the log books with detailed references to source and date. This text is lodged with the museum in case any later researcher wants to check but for the sake of readability the references have been removed. Everything quoted in chapters 3 to 6 comes from the log books unless otherwise stated.

For any reader who has not visited the Braintree museum, please do so, some of the artefacts showing the ethos and traditions of the school are very visible as part of the building. It is difficult to visualise the school in action except in its latter years when photography was much easier. There is now a mezzanine floor in the main school room and this along with the large and very interesting show cases take away the sense of space that the room had when in use as a school. There are regular re-enactments of Victorian and other periods of education, which are very popular with visiting schools. These take place in one of the rooms of the 1911 extension, not the large original school room. Sadly, the combination of changes in the National Curriculum and increased transport costs prevent schools from coming in any number. With a bit of imagination and a few of the illustrations of what it might have looked like, it is well worth standing in the building and considering some of the activities and events that have taken place.

This is not just an account of the use of a building but of lives. It might be possible to make a rough estimate from the log book of the number of children and young people who were educated in the school over the years but given the uncertainty of how long any individual actually stayed in the school, it is not really a worthwhile task. Anything from two hundred to four hundred pupils were on roll in any year just in the junior school. Adding in the infant numbers must bring it to nearly 600 children on site at some dates. Ages varied, the separate managers' accounts and log books for the two schools while they existed, confuses the issue further. It is possible to list the headteachers but not the many teachers. Supporting staff, who certainly in latter years outnumbered the teaching staff, are rarely mentioned. We have put a brief list of the main statistics at the end along with an annotated time line with the main historical events taking place in the wider world which must have influenced the life and teaching in the school.

One of the newspaper accounts of the opening ceremony from the Braintree and Bocking Advertiser April 16th 1862 Photo 1.10 states that:

> 'The opening of the Braintree Public Schools, the particulars of which we give today, is an event, the importance of which, in its relation to the future welfare and general prosperity of the town, cannot be exceeded. There are also, in the manner in which this noble building has been given to the, 'poorer classes of this town and neighbourhood, considerations which greatly increase its value, being not only an example of munificence but in its purposes and disposition, teaching all men the high objects upon which their time and energies should be spent and the liberal, large hearted and catholic spirit which Should unite them in their work.'

A theme of benevolence, quality of purpose and non sectarian liberalism permeates the story. The school may have been intended for children of poorer people but the philosophy of teaching and learning professed by the staff was one of high expectations allied with care and understanding. The culture of the school was such that for many, working at the school was a way of life, their loyalty was intense. Teaching staff came unmarried, left and returned in later life. Ex-pupils became members of staff both teaching and support staff. Most pupils went on to successful lives with a good grounding. Those we have spoken to have many fond memories even where tinged with critical or sad ones. The modern media of Facebook is voicing some of these.

Underlying all the warm feelings are some more sad and unpleasant ones and that is evident from the beginning of the school. The opening ceremony was tinged with sadness, the original benefactor having died before the opening. The building, so greatly admired at that ceremony, proved not to be ideal for purpose, due to limitations of ventilation, heating, sanitation and play space and these proved to be reasons for the eventual closure. Throughout all of any institution's history, relationships will not always be good, in any school some individual pupils will have had bad educational experiences and outside circumstances will affect how happy or effective any organisation can be. Some of these will necessarily be touched upon.

END NOTES

[1] Curtis reckoned there was probably less literacy than in Tudor times Curtis, 1967

[2] Mike Baker's account of schools in Braintree gives some local details Baker, 1981

[3] The manor was given to Ralph de Marci soon after the Norman conquest Bardell, 1996

[4] BBC, 2010 08 02 10

Chapter 2 The beginning 1861–1862

The trust deeds and the accounts of the opening ceremony show what an unusual foundation the school had. There was a clear vision of education as seen by the founders which resonates right through the subsequent history of elementary education today. The original fragile copies of the Braintree and Bocking Advertiser for 1862 contain long descriptions of the building itself on April 9th and the ceremony on April 16th. Photo 2.1

Mr. S. Clement Ryley MA JP an early scholar at the school, donated a hardboard mounted cutting from the second date, to the school in 1926. Mr. Ryley later became vice Chairman of Dorset Education Committee. A full typescript of the 5,000 word account is in Braintree Museum. No modern school opening would warrant such an account. Photo 2.2

It starts:

> *'The formal opening of the handsome and commodious schoolroom recently erected in Manor Street, Braintree for the use of the Braintree Public School and the proceedings declaratory of their being a gift for the use of the children of the poorer classes of this town and neighbourhood, by the late George Courtauld of Bocking took place on Monday evening the 7th instant under the able presidency of the Rev. Sir John Page Wood Bart.'*[1] Photo 2.4

This may have been called a public school but it was not a school like Rugby or Eton, more generally thought of as Public Schools, it was to be a school for the public, particularly those who could not afford the private schools that were then available. The building was certainly handsome and still is. The Rev. Sir John Page Wood was for many years vicar of Cressing. He was married to Emma Michell, a woman of great energy and versatility who won renown as a talented artist and successful novelist.[2]

> *'The unsectarian principles on which the institution is based and the liberality of the provisions of the trust deed, render it, in addition to its architectural features, which are of a very high character, a gift worthy of the acceptance of the town and the appreciation of all who are interested in the education of youth. It will also remain an enduring memorial to the worth of the late benevolent founder, whose sympathies were ever strong in favour of institutions which had for their object the education of people. The cost of the present building was £2,200, which in addition to the sum of £1,000 as an endowment was the sole gift of the late George Courtauld Esq. The intentions,*

29

Photo 2.1 Newspaper cuttings mounted on hardboard reporting opening ceremony. Braintree and Bocking Times 16 04 1862.

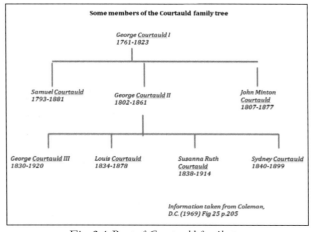

Photo 2.2 Donor of cuttings also on hardboard.

Some members of the Courtauld family tree

George Courtauld I
1761-1823

Samuel Courtauld
1793-1881

George Courtauld II
1802-1861

John Minton
Courtauld
1807-1877

George Courtauld III
1830-1920

Louis Courtauld
1834-1878

Susanna Ruth
Courtauld
1838-1914

Sydney Courtauld
1840-1899

Information taken from Coleman,
D.C. (1969) Fig 25 p.205

Fig. 2.1 Part of Courtauld family tree

aims and hopes of the deceased gentleman, as regards the present erection, were as will be seen below, lucidly explained by the eldest son who bears his name.'[3] Photo 2.2 & Photo 2.3

The late George Courtauld mentioned, was the younger brother of Samuel. Both were sons of George Courtauld, 1761-1823, who founded Courtaulds textile firm. By 1850, Samuel employed over 2,000 people in his three silk mills and he had recruited partners including, in 1828, his brother. Sadly, the benefactor George had died the year before the school was opened and it was his son George who performed the opening ceremony. Fig. 2.1

Using an internet calculator, the school as a project in 2016 would have an economic cost of £5,064,000 to build with a labour cost of £1,429,000. From internet research, these are comparable costs to building a new primary school in 2016. Similarly, the endowment of £1,000 of 1860 represents a prestige value of £1,029,000 or an economic investment value of £2,302,000 in 2016.[4]

The newspaper article lists the important people present.

There were several other members of the Courtauld family although not Samuel, the more senior one, J. M. Courtauld Esq., Miss E Courtauld, Miss S R. Courtauld, Louis Courtauld Esq., Sidney Courtauld Esq. and other names presumably well known to the readers of the newspaper. S W. Saville Esq., John S. Harrison Esq. and Mrs. Harrison, John Harrison Esq. Jun. Rev., Thomas Craig and Mrs. Craig, Augustus

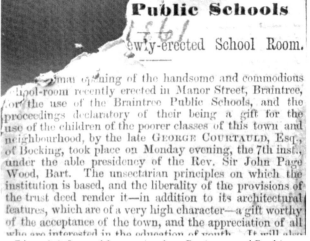

Public Schools

newly-erected School Room.

...the opening of the handsome and commodious school-room recently erected in Manor Street, Braintree, for the use of the Braintree Public Schools, and the proceedings declaratory of their being a gift for the use of the children of the poorer classes of this town and neighbourhood, by the late GEORGE COURTAULD, Esq., of Bocking, took place on Monday evening, the 7th inst., under the able presidency of the Rev. Sir John Page Wood, Bart. The unsectarian principles on which the institution is based, and the liberality of the provisions of the trust deed render it—in addition to its architectural features, which are of a very high character—a gift worthy of the acceptance of the town, and the appreciation of all who are interested in the education of youth. It will also

Photo 2.3 Start of first cutting from Braintree and Bocking Times 16.04.1862

Cunnington Esq., Mrs. Craig and family, Davidson Esq. and Mrs Davidson, H Le Keux Esq., Charles Tabor Esq., and family, Rev. J. Robertson, Mrs. Ash, Mrs. Smart, Henry Hobbs Esq. and family, Thomas Taylor Esq., Mrs. Clench, John Gosling and family.[5]

The next part of the report is of the musical entertainment that made up part of the evening, an insight into the kind of social activity that Victorian people enjoyed at this time. The Mr. James Dace mentioned below was the founder of the firm James Dace and Son in Chelmsford, a firm still well known for their sales of music and musical instruments including pianos. James was a local musician and well established teacher who started the shop just off London Road in Chelmsford in 1852.

'A selection of music was admirably sung by the Misses Fitzwalter and Emily Millar and Messrs Trelawny Cobham and Charles Chaple, the entertainment being under the direction of Mr. Dace of Chelmsford, who ably presided at the pianoforte. The selection included a duet, I know a bank, which was sung by Miss Fitzwalter and Miss Millar and elicited enthusiastic cheers and encores. The duet Excelsior by Mr. Cobham and Mr. Chaple and the song, The village blacksmith, were also especially admired and applauded. We believe it was generally acknowledged to be a rich musical treat.'[6] When the school celebrated the 125th anniversary in 1987, they did so by performing a pageant of the history and started with a scene from the opening ceremony based on this account. Photo 2.4

Photo 2.4 1987, scene from pageant rehearsal of children re-enacting the opening ceremony.

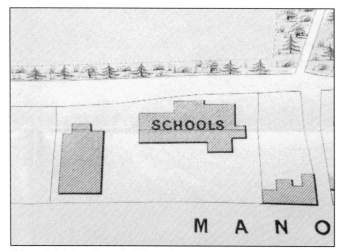

Photo 2.5 Map of two buildings shown on map in auctioneer's details for the sale of Mount House Estate

The Chairman made a long speech, despite declaring he was not very well. The death of the benefactor George Courtauld meant his son George had to make the main speech, another long one. Various other people also had their say including the then head teacher. It could have been a scene out of Dickens. In the 21st century we find these kinds of eulogies difficult to digest. They talk of the spiritual as well as intellectual and social needs. They also comment on the variety of types of schools available in Britain at that time and the unusual character of the proposed school. Manor Street School was unusual in its founding ethos. The state only supported existing schools through grants dependent on the results of inspection. The churches, Anglican, Roman Catholic and non-conformist, being the main providers of schools for the middle and upper lower classes, all took the opportunity to indoctrinate the children in their particular ways of worship.

The Courtaulds were of Huguenot origin and Unitarian by faith, giving the rationale for their public works and founding this school in particular. They wanted to help others in a non-sectarian way. Christianity was still a dominant theme in people's lives in the mid nineteenth century even if church or chapel attendance was more of an expected ritual than the result of deeply held faith. Darwin was only beginning his work, questioning orthodox doctrine was not popular. Even though the industrial revolution was well underway. materialism had not had the impact it now has. The class structure was seen as inevitable, everyone had a place, even the poor .

The school as an organisation had been functioning for some time, this was just a new building for it, hence the past tense in the following passage.

> *'In this school there appeared to be nothing sectarian, it had the support of an enlightened and liberal government and in it was read the bible, without note or comment, unadulterated and unmutilated. Children were expected by their parents, in this school, to be brought up in the nurture and admonition of the Lord. The course marked out by the noble founder for carrying on in this school appeared to him to be the most judicious one.'7*

The speaker commented on the founding of The Literary and Mechanics Institute which was established in Halstead in 1843 with its first president, Samuel Courtauld. ERO, 1846-1918.

It established a lending library and paid a librarian, organised lectures, entertainments and excursions, even attracting a small government grant. The attendees were Master tradesmen and others, including women, ladies, 'not of the working classes.' George Courtauld also the next year, 1862, presented Braintree with its own Institute at Bocking End, also designed by the same architect as the school, Mr. Stock of London. [8] The school was seen as another example of the philanthropic nature of the Courtauld family and also their egalitarian outlook and interest in education in its widest meaning. Photo 2.6

It is clear from the following extract that the proposed secular ethos of the school had not been fully understood by local people and even when understood, was viewed with some suspicion.

Mr. George Courtauld then rose and said, Sir John Wood, Ladies and gentlemen, it devolves upon me and not perhaps unnaturally, to explain to you as lucidly and briefly as I may, the plan, scope, intention and general character of the school the opening of this new building we are met to commemorate and I hope that before I sit down, I shall be able to correct certain errors and allay certain apprehensions, which I understand to be entertained in some quarters respecting both the ends we have in view and the means whereby we seek to gain them. And the chief, and I might say

Photo 2.6 Braintree Institute, Bocking End.

the only reason which induced us to have this public opening was that we might set ourselves right, as it were by placing our school before them in its true light and giving them, as a basis for their judgement plain fact, instead of what we have reason to believe has been erroneous representation. [9]

The background to the founding of the school

You are most of you aware that for some years past a considerable school has been conducted on these premises which went by various names. Some people called it the Manor Road School, others the Public Training School and others again, Mr. Rees' School, this last no doubt from the fact that during his residence in this neighbourhood the Rev. Mr. Rees took a great and active interest in the school and the fact that it was used until recently as a Sunday School by the children over which Mr. Rees was minister. It is right to state that from the first, the instruction given in the day school was as absolutely undoctrinal as it is now and that the conditions and management of the school were then almost as precisely similar to what they are now, the property of the school, being then, as now, vested in trustees and its management being in the hands of a committee. [10]

The Revd. David Rees was the Braintree Baptist Church minister from 1845 and had left in 1859 to live in Geelong, Australia. This left the church with interregnum ministers at the time of the opening. There is no reference to an existing Sunday school in the church minutes of the time but a new schoolroom adjoining the chapel was erected and opened on October 1st 1862. The church had however, been given £40 to relinquish the use of the old school Building.

Governance and finances

George continues talking about his father's interest and support for the existing school.

From almost the first, my father had taken a deep interest in the school, most thoroughly recognising and approving the principle of the total absence of all doctrinal teaching and being himself instrumental in establishing it on such a broad and catholic basis. This interest of his increased with its increasing prosperity and usefulness and from time to time spent considerable sums in repairing, refitting and adding to the premises and supplemented from his own purse by far the greater portion of the deficit that each year showed between the receipts on the one hand, in the way of children's pence and government grant, for the school had been placed under government inspection and expenditure on the other. [11]

Government grants were rarely the major source of school's income, their importance was they made the difference between insolvency and debt.[12]   Clearly in the case of this school it didn't make a sufficient difference. George Courtauld senior had had to bail them out .

And now let me say a few words as to our present position and the condition of our trust. This building, with the surrounding premises and the piece of ground on the opposite side of the road, which we intend for the present to use as a playground and upon which we may possibly in some future time build a house for the master, together with the sum of, £1,000 for the purpose of founding a small endowment. [13]

Although the committee was the nationally understood form of governance, the founder wanted his principles of co-operation to be part of the school's ethos. A donation of £5 is equivalent in 2016 to £415, real price, or related to labour value, £3,247, quite a substantial sum. Even an annual subscription of 10 shillings, 50p of our money, would have been worth £30, real price or, £324, earnings related, quite a sum if asked of people today to fund a new school.

And first it is conditioned that the management of the school should be by a committee, during his life my father's tendencies in all these matters were essentially cooperative. [14]

George quotes from the trust deed detail, *the committee of management is to consist of twelve persons to be annually elected, seven of whom shall be chose by the trustees and donors of not less than five pounds each and annual subscribers of not less than ten shillings each, by a majority of votes of such electoral body of trustees, donors and subscribers and the remaining five members of the committee to be chosen by the parents of the children for the time being in the school and the first duty of such committee upon election, shall be to appoint a committee of ladies consisting of not more that twelve, whose province it shall be to exercise all necessary supervision over the girls in the school and especially the infant school and who shall be entitled to vote in all committee meetings, that is to say committee meetings whereat the ladies are present together with and at the request of the original committee.* [15]

To have members of the committee chosen by parents was advanced and George Farmer's version added that, *'it was found to work remarkably well in the past.'* But it was only in the 1970s and 1980s, when governing bodies were being reformed, that it became law for all governing bodies to have parent representation. Here however, these were not parents themselves necessarily but elected by the parents. The committee of ladies is also interesting, albeit they were subservient to the men and only responsible for the girls or infants, at least they were involved and girls were being educated.

It may appear to you strange that five out of the twelve members should be chosen by the parents of the children and doubtless such an arrangement is very uncommon, if not absolutely singular but I think the principle is good. I think it is a good thing to give the parents some voice in the control and management of the schools to which they send their children, thus of course giving them a greater interest in the school. With regard to the usefulness of the subcommittee, rather I should say the committee of ladies, it is quite evident that there might constantly arise in connexion with the arrangements for and the management of girls and infants, in which the advice and assistance of ladies would be of the greatest service. [16]

Teaching and learning

Given the prevailing insistence on religious education and examination in the 3Rs, this proposed curriculum is wide and enlightened.

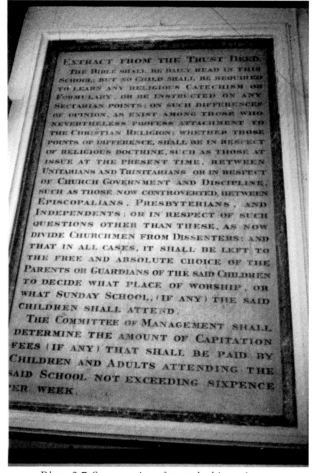

Photo 2.7 Stone version of trust deed in main room.

> *And it is hereby declared that the instruction of the said school shall comprise at least reading, writing and arithmetic, English grammar, geography, natural and general history and the elements of the physical sciences and besides in the case of girls', needlework.*

> *Such is the quality of instruction that, at least, we are bound to give and I should here state that it is the province of the committee to determine the capitation fee, that is the sum that is to be paid by each pupil but that in no case is such sum to exceed 6d per week.* [17]

The non sectarian approach to the curriculum, is set out in great detail by the speaker. This certainly is distinctive. The unique characteristics of the Unitarian church are not often recognised today. In Victorian times the mainstream Christian Churches put a lot of emphasis on the threefold nature of their belief, the Trinity of the Father, God, the son, Jesus and the Holy Ghost or Holy Spirit. Unitarians emphasise the singularity of God and are often seen as on the liberal wing of Christian belief. The Courtaulds wanted no doctrinal teaching of either variety but just wanted the bible readings to speak for themselves.

> *And now I come to the distinctive character of our school and which more than any other I wish to explain clearly and fully. I mean the total absence of all doctrinal religious teaching. Allow me to read an extract from the trust deed, a copy of which appears on the tablet on yonder wall and which I think will convince you that we are as absolutely forbidden to teach Unitarianism as we are Trinitarianism and it is hereby further declared that the Bible shall be daily read in the said school but no child shall be required to learn any religious catechism or formulary, or be instructed on any sectarian points, on such differences of opinion as exist among those who never the less profess attachment to the Christian religion, whether those points of difference shall be in respect of religious*

doctrine and that in all cases it shall be left to the free and absolute choice of the parents or guardians of the said children to decide what place of worship or what Sunday School, if any. [18] *Photo 2.7*

Photo 2.8 Feed my lambs, on gable end of building

Local people had obviously thought that absence of doctrine would mean absence of religious teaching so George tries to explain the difference. Most schools today would welcome a statement similar to the one given here in bold as part of their mission statement.

'We will educate them, draw out, that is the power of their minds, we teach them to think and supply them with subjects for thought and more than this if you send your children to our school we trust and believe you will find there a good wholesome tone of truth and honour and probity, it is from yourselves at home, it is from your ministers in church or chapel, it is from the teachers in your Sunday Schools, that they must receive that direct and doctrinal religious teaching that you wish impressed upon them.' [19]

There is still confusion in many people's minds over the difference between religious and spiritual instruction. Religious instruction is required of state schools, children learn about Judaism, Islam, Buddhism and other religions as well as the tenets of the various strands of the Christian faith. However, an emphasis on spiritual awareness through art, music or science does tend to be less obvious or considered.

The building itself

George describes the building and its architect.

'He, George Courtauld Senior, saw two plans which the architect had drawn out for this new building, chose the one he thought most suitable and drew up a long list of suggestions and instructions in detail for the guidance of the architect and builder and it was he who selected from St. John's Gospel the beautiful and pregnant sentence which appears cut in stone on our principal gable. Feed my Lambs.' Photo 2.8

'The architect was Mr. Stock of London and the builder our fellow townsman, Mr Brown and I think I may say, without exaggeration, that their labours have resulted in a school room than which a more commodious one does not exist in this county of Essex.' [20]

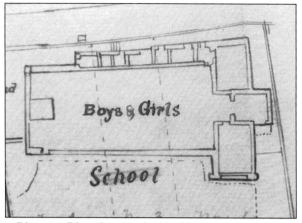

Photo 2.9 Plan of 1861 school building taken from 1895 deeds of transfer to school board

There is an elegant description of the building in the earlier newspaper cutting and a good layout plan in the 1895 deeds.

'From the centre of this roof rises a very elegant and graceful bell turret, surmounted by a spire with a gilded final finial. The building is faced with red bricks lightened by Bath stone dressing.

The front grounds are laid out with a green lawn and planted with shrubs, the whole being enclosed with a very chaste wall of brick and stone surmounted by a horizontal iron fence.

The main schoolroom is 71 feet long and 33 feet wide and about 20 feet high to the centre of the ceiling which is plastered white and is made in the form of an ellipse supported by arched timber ribs. These continue a little way down the walls and are supported on stone corbels, being left exposed they are stained and varnished and for a pleasing relief to the appearance of the ceiling. The side walls are covered with a fine stucco of a warm buff colour which produces very softening effecting the aspect of the room. In addition to this there is a gallery classroom, 21 feet by 13 feet and a committee room about the same size having in it cupboards containing the library belonging to the school. There is also a lobby, 15 feet by 11 feet which gives as the entrance to the main room and is fitted up with hat and cap rails and pegs for the use of the children. In addition to these at the back are the necessary offices, coal stores and furnace room. The whole of the rooms are heated by hot water apparatus and lighted by rows of star light gas burners, this part of the work being executed by Mr. F. B. Crittall of Braintree. The main room is well ventilated by two of Watson's patent syphon ventilators.' Photo 2.9

Photo 2.10 Warley Hospital, Brentwood.

Mr. Stock, 1824 or 25 to 1909, is known to the Royal Institute of British Architects. He was a district surveyor in east London, later a county surveyor for Essex, as well as architect and surveyor to the Haberdasher Company for 23 years. He was responsible amongst other things and Manor School, for Young's Brewery at Wandsworth, Hay's Wharf,

Haberdashers School at New Cross, Rotherhithe Public Library, Haberdashers Aske's School at Acton*, West Hampstead, an enlargement of Peek Frean Co's biscuit factories in Bermondsey, science and art buildings for Monmouth Grammar School and an extension of Essex County Lunatic Asylum, Brentwood, now Warley Hospital, Brentwood. email Peter Kent, RIBA Information Centre, January 8th 2009.[21] Photo 2.10

Some other speakers

After Mr. George Courtauld finished speaking, Mr. Clench, the committee secretary, said:

As honorary secretary he had been desired to lay before them several particulars regarding the statistical and financial position of the school ... At the present time the number of children was 210, the average attendance 182. Of the former number, 151 belonged to the mixed school and 59 were infants ... So, it would be seen that their prospects were that the expenditure would exceed the income by about, £50. They had also by the liberality of their late patron been enabled to establish a library in connexion with the schools, which now numbered 271 vols. Their connection too with the Government was of a very pleasing kind, not only on account of the capitation grant but also on account of the schools being periodically examined by one of Her Majesty's inspectors, the result of which was afterwards made known to the committee and parents by a report from the Committee of Council on Education. [22]*

The Committee of Council on Education is what subsequently became the government Department of Education. The Revised code's infamous payment by results, seems to have benefitted Manor as the inspectors had reported favourably.

The master and mistress also, in addition to their salaries, had payments made to them which were regulated by their success in teaching. Thus they were entitled to obtain more qualified teachers than they could otherwise.

There were four pupil teachers in the school, each receiving salaries from the government. It was the intention of the managers to hold a public meeting once a year in order to lay before them a general report of the school. Respecting the estimated deficit, the committee sincerely hoped that persons who were not yet subscribers would become so and aid the work so nobly commenced. Loud cheers.

Mr. John Saunders, Teacher of the School , next addressed the meeting at considerable length. in the course of which he paid a merited tribute to the character of the late Mr. Courtauld with whom for some years he had been personally acquainted. He spoke also of the beauty and completeness of the building and of the necessity in order to make its use thoroughly successful of the parents giving their encouragement and support to the teacher.

He concluded by expressing his joy at seeing so many friends and relations of the departed present this evening, thus evincing the fact that they sanctioned the motives which led to the erection and from which the hope might probably be indulged, that they would be the first to interest themselves in its future success. Cheers.

Mr. Henry Everard, as a parent of the scholars, spoke in terms of high commendation of the character of the instruction afforded to the scholars.[23] After various votes of thanks and acknowledgements, the meeting concluded by the National Anthem being sung.'[24]

How many meetings today would end with the singing of the National Anthem?

END NOTES

[1] Anon, 1862

[2] Bradhurst, 2009

[3] Anon, 1862

[4] Lawrence and Williamson, 2016

[5] Families of some of these people may still live in Braintree. Anon, 1862

[6] Anon, 1862

[7] Anon,1862

[8] Bettley and Pevsner, 2007

[9] Anon, 1862

[10] Anon, 1862

[11] Anon 1862

[12] Ball, 1893 p.78

[13] Anon, 1862

[14] Anon, 1862

[15] Anon,1862

[16] Anon, 1862

[17] Anon,1862

[18] Anon, 1862

[19] Anon, 1862

[20] Anon,1862

[21] Those in the list marked with an asterisk can be seen by typing the names into Google.

[22] Anon, 1862

[23] Anon, 1862

[24] Anon, 1862

Chapter 3 The early years 1862-1882

Braintree continued to develop as an industrial town set in a very rural situation aided by the coming of the railway. It was the age of Gladstone and Disraeli battling it out over possible reforms, more sectors of the populace got the vote. It was also an era of increasing thought being given to social justice. Universities became more open and there was an increased freedom of thought. Darwin's Origin of Species had been published in 1859. Ideas of Britain as a global power, the growth of the empire and the increased mechanization of industry meant there was less demand for crude labour and more demand for people who could read and write.

Governance

The hotly debated Forster Act of 1870 introduced local school boards. The school boards, the first local education authorities, were directly elected by ratepayers by a system of proportional representation. The boards provided the extra schools but also had powers to introduce and to enforce compulsory attendance at all schools, voluntary and board.[1] This was not to be free education nor universal provision, parents would be requested to pay up to 9d a week although those unable to pay would be allowed to attend free. The boards would decide the nature, i.e. the denominational flavour, of the religious instruction and parents were given the right to withdraw their children from this if they wished.

The school, received notice that the school is now and in the future to be under the School Board on 9th February 1876.[2]

On this date, the master also gives details of the finances of the school at that time.

Grants. attendance 174 @ 6s. *6 shillings = 30p* £52 4s. 0d. *£52 20p.*
  Exam qual. 172

Presented 160
Passed reading, 153⎫
    writing. 123 ⎬ 416 @ 3s.
             3 shillings = 15p
    arith. . . 140⎭
In classes 172 at 4s. *4 shillings = 20p*

Specific subjects 172 at 4/-
  £103.4s.0 = *£103.20*
P T grant
  £7.0s.0d
Fees made up
  £162.8s.0 = *£162.40*
40 children debtors.

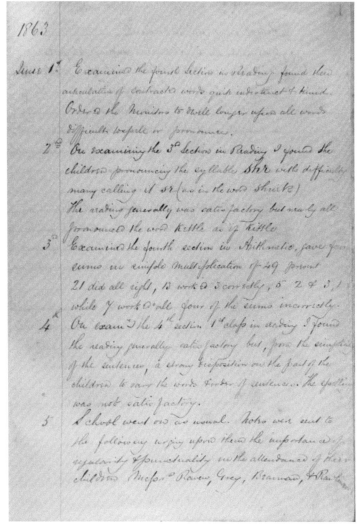

Photo 3.1 First page of first junior log book.

Manor Street was not the only school open at the time, St. Michael's, the church school, opened during the first few years of Manor's life. 'New church schools opened which compete with this school,' is recorded in 1867. According to Quin,[3] the school board mentioned operated solely for Manor; the Anglican National school, St. Michael's, opted to remain outside the board. This was not so in Bocking where their board governed five schools. Braintree School Board was set up two years after the Bocking board. Its members were Mr. Sidney Courtauld, one of the trustees at the time of the transfer of power, the Rev. Thomas Cartright, the Rev. Albert Goodrich, Mr. Henry Horsnaill and Mr. Frederick West; Mr. E. Holmes was the board secretary. The trustees George and Sidney Courtauld offered the school on very generous terms to the board, a nominal rent of £1 a year to be paid by the board along with a yearly endowment of £40. They left in place the condition that no higher fee than 6d should be paid for any pupil.

The board resolved that a sliding scale of fees should operate.

Anyone not in receipt of a weekly wage, i.e. on a salary, should pay the full rate, otherwise for the children over 6 years old it would be 3d and if two or more children came from the same family 2d and infants, younger than 6, it would also be 2d. Quin also mentions that reading the minutes of the school board gives yet another set of insights into the social conditions of the age, how difficult it was for families to manage if the father and main breadwinner of the family was ill, dead or in the local workhouse or if no work was available for the adults; children were leaving to go to work in the mills aged 12. The board minutes also give the staff salaries, the master was to be paid, £175 a year, the assistant mistress, £75 a year, two of the four pupil teachers £15 a year,

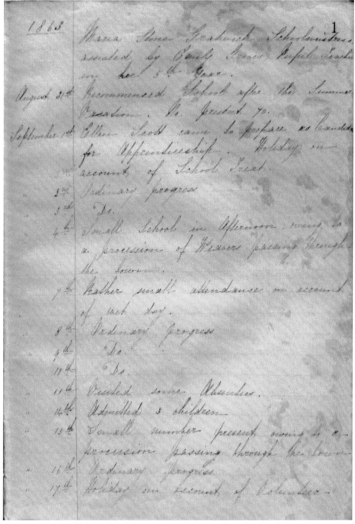

Photo 3.2 First page of first infant log book.

the other two £10 a year, in all £300 a year. This doesn't tie up with the income stated by the master, maybe staff salaries came from some other pot.

People

Headteachers

The general picture conveyed at the beginning of Manor, is one of a master, Mr Saunders, in charge of the junior or main school, with pupil teachers, referred to by him in the log books as PTs, some monitors, even younger than the PTs and a mistress in charge of the infants. She also had some additional young adult help. Mrs. Saunders, presumably the master's wife, was noted as in charge of sewing and Arthur Gunnell was noted as the PT in an inspection in 1864. Children were transferred from the infants to the juniors, at least on one occasion, in November, 1865 'Rec'd children from infant school as usual.'

Mr. Saunders went into the ministry when he left the school and 1868 saw a new master, Mr. GH Matthews, who resigned in June 1873. Whether the HMI visit in October of that year was at the end of Mr. Matthews' time at the school or with a new master is not clear but the visit was a disaster, it is reminiscent of some schools' reports of the early days of Ofsted.

'The annual visit of HMI, which was of such an unusual character that I report it here at length.

From the moment the inspector entered the room till the moment he left he indulged in a wholesale course of fault finding and blame and that in such an ungenerous and uncharitable manner as must have a very disheartening influence on the master and assistants. To none or nothing was awarded the smallest medium of praise though it is evident to all who take an interest in the schools that a great improvement in every direction has been effected.

The master desires to record that during the whole of his professional life he has never been subjected to such ungenerous and ungentlemanly conduct at the hand of an inspector before.

From such a depressing and repressive visit the only effect can be a most injurious one to the teachers and children and from the nature and circumstances of the visit will be a long remembered one. The inspector was the Rev. Robinson, 1873.'

The first entry for the infant log book was August 31st 1863, when the school, commenced after the summer vacation, 'No. present 70.' Photo 3.2

Photo 3.3 Imaginary sketch of possible scene in large schoolroom with teacher, monitors, pupil teachers and pupils.

The head of the infants, known as the school mistress then, was Maria Stone Gatwick, with Emily Groves as her pupil teacher. Despite this, the early log records that the school was under the master's supervision, from 1869 to 1873. There was a bit of a problem with the teacher, Eliza Wicks, taking the youngest in the infant room, because she was not certified, only Mr. Matthews, a master at that time, was. The concern was that he was in a separate room and, 'my Lords cannot regard the infant school as under the immediate instruction of Mr. Matthews but so long as the average number of infants in this room does not exceed 40.'

This is also referred to later in an HMI report of December 1871.

'The infant room is too far off to admit the master's superintendence, recommends that the infant school should be carried on as a separate department.'

'My Lords were prepared to recognise Eliza and make separate returns for the infant school. She seems well fitted to her work and when old enough should try for a certificate.'

No one completed the infant log book for this time. It seems the school managing committee were usually referred to as 'My Lords' despite not being lords of the realm.

The log book records that from 1871 onwards the infant school was to be run as a separate entity. It remained as such until 1952, with separate log books, inspections and buildings. There was quite a series of mistresses from 1873 onwards but this seemed to settle down about the time Mr. Davies took over the juniors in 1882.

Monitors

The monitorial system had been introduced in the early part of the nineteenth century. The headteacher would split the large number of pupils into smaller groups, each to be taught by a monitor. The master would meet his monitors every day before school and teach them what they had in turn to pass on to the children. When school began the teacher, in theory, had only to supervise.[4] They were paid pence a day. A rather confused entry in the junior log book states:

> 'I have tried a weekly trial of monitors by a daily trial of them, paying them proportionally less, I find it very difficult to get boys sufficiently interested in their work to enable the teacher to depend on them. I am doubtful whether I shall continue last Monday's plan of stopping the whole school to collect pence. Boys with nothing to do are very difficult to keep quiet.'

It is hard to understand what the role of the monitors actually played from this but not hard to understand the master's problem with unoccupied boys. Photo 3.3

Pupil teachers

Pupil teachers were introduced in England in 1846 and were in effect apprentices, paid out of government funds. They had to be at least thirteen when they were appointed, they would serve for five years and would be able to compete for Queen's scholarships. These entitled successful candidates to up to three years training at the colleges which were being established by the religious denominations. This was the beginning of the end of the monitorial system.[5]

Manor School seemed to be running both systems together in its early years. One entry states, 'the pupil teachers very slow and dull in consequence more work and worry is thrown upon the master than is good for him.'

and another,

'Compelled to reprimand, for his dilatory habits and pointed out the necessity for greater vivacity, life and energy when managing his class.' also: 'PTs are careless about pencils.' and 'Working till after 9 o'c at night in consequence of work from report. PTs and master.'

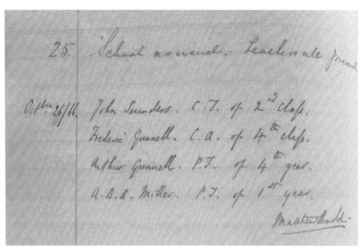

Photo 3.4 Matthew Arnold's signature from junior log book 1866

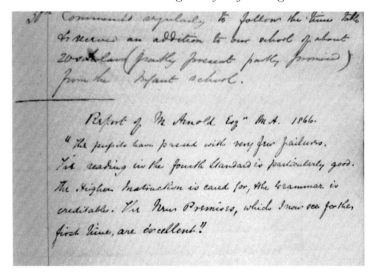

Photo 3.5 Matthew Arnold's report entered in the log book by the headteacher 1866

Teachers

Teachers were certificated, that is, they had passed an examination at the end of a full time course of training or as practicing teachers had passed an external examination and were paid for their time in teaching pupil teachers.[6] Annie Llewellyn was said to be, on supply, when she was a second year student from Stockwell Training College.

The Revised Code of 1862 brought in the system of payment by results. Children were to be submitted for examination in standards and a strict schedule in each of these subjects, the three Rs, was laid down for each subject.[7] It led to more rote learning and teaching to the tests. This all sounds rather familiar even in the second decade of the 21st century.

Inspectors and inspection

Some of the inspectors' comments are included from time to time in the log books but in general they inspected registers and checked the number present so that the school could be paid on its results, attendance results not academic ones and its buildings.

The infant school was inspected by a Mr. Anderson HMI, on 24.06.63 and Matthew Arnold HMI on 26.10.66, 17.10.67 and 21.10.68. Photos 3.4 & 3.5

The junior school was inspected on the same dates as the infants.

'Superintending monitor of lowest section given orders not to hurry or omit bits of lessons.'

'The pupils have passed with very few failures. In reading the fourth standard is particularly good. The Higher Instruction is cared for, the grammar is creditable. The new premises which I now see for the first time, are excellent.'

'The needlework improved but it is desirable that a Ladies Committee should visit regularly, not seldomer than once a month, to receive the report of the sewing mistress on this work and inspect it.'

'Articles 53 a and b, are not satisfied in the case of the boys' school. Article 53 saves the school from a deduction under 52 b.'

Matthew Arnold is much more well known now as a poet and critic but had had to work as a school inspector to earn a living. As an inspector, he was a staunch advocate of both universal and state education even though he complained about the strain of working in this way to enable him to write. He visited schools in Europe as well as England and was highly critical of the payment by results system for which he was providing evidence. Payment by results would lead to cutbacks which would lower standards. The proposal treated school as a mere machine for teaching rather than a living whole with complex functions, religious moral and intellectual.[8] He apparently came close to losing his job or any hope of promotion because of his championing the fate of lower class children but was held in great affection by teachers and students who had dealings with him.[9]

The Lords of the committee visited and signed the log books as did Her Majesty's Inspectorate, HMI. The master defers to the lords, or at least the chairman, Mr. G. Courtauld in things like, 'a thorough change of reading books.' This sounds very like the current system of referring to a chair of Governors for expenditure over a certain amount rather than about asking advice on the choice of text.

'Boys gave an evening of entertainment and G. Courtauld presided.' Miss Crittall and Mrs. Courtauld, along with the Rev. Cartwright, are recorded in the infant log books as visiting every few months. They seem mainly to check the registers against the number actually present.

It appears that the school was inspected by members of the Board after it came under its aegis, 'because the head in 1881, objects to an examination of deformed boy, asked class 6X to stand up but looks the same up as down.'

'Sec. of Board objected to objection in log book.'

'Master then queried exam. of children, good children not passing, vice versa.'

'Again Sec. of Board *objects to, above reflections.*'

On December 23rd this head, a Mr. Rose, resigns and in the January of the following year a new head. R.N. Davies, takes up the post, start of a long headship of which more in the next chapter.

The children

It is difficult to ascertain the ages of the children attending either school and there is no real indication of how many children in total came to the school over the years it was open. It appears from general research that even quite young children, maybe as young as two years old may have attended and references to the babies' room probably means just this. Certainly, there is a reference to some being admitted under 3 years old, having previously mentioned putting some five and half year old who, 'can neither write from the simplest copy nor do anything else, with the three year old babies.' How the staff coped with children in nappies, or with the sort of play and sleep provision we recognise as needed for such nursery age children is unclear. It is not at all clear at this time how far the infant school just child minded or what kind of curriculum or methodology the school had. One child is recorded as having left the infant school, thus under 8 years old, to, 'mind her mother's baby.'

One amazing contribution to the writing of this book has been the reminiscence of a pupil of that time, William Pannell, which we were able to read, William was born in 1855 and his memoirs are being published by his family. William started school in his own village until man enough to walk 2 miles to Braintree to the Manor Street School, which had been "built and endowed by George Courtauld. I think I was about 8 and very rarely missed a day, John Saunders was headmaster and 2 other masters." Saunders afterwards went for the ministry and became minister to the Jacket Street Congregational Church, Ipswich. "The day before breaking up school for Xmas 1867 saw a notice in the window of John Dyer, a respectable lad wanted, the next morning at breaking up and prize distribution. I happened to be a prize winner, was called onto the platform and handed the prize by George Courtauld with a kindly word. Was bucked up a bit with my prize and plucked up the courage to go to see Mr. Dyer".

William showed Mr. Dyer his prize. He opened the cover and read, "for good conduct and progress in arithmetic" and William described his work at Bulford Mill on Saturdays. He went for a trial to be a bound apprentice for four years. His indenture papers to be apprenticed in the art of a grocer, are also part of the Watkinson, not the author, family archive.

While grades or standards are referred to, it is not clear to what ages the children stayed on until at Manor. The factory acts allowed children of over eight years old to be employed for a few hours provided the children could produce a certificate to prove they were undertaking at least some form of schooling. 'Admitted several part time girls from Mr. Waters' factory.' They could be fully employed from thirteen onwards. The factory acts influenced schooling availability more than any education act at the time. Braintree Union, founded in 1835, established a workhouse in Rayne Road for 'in relief', as well as administering 'out relief.' The workhouse later became St. Michael's Hospital, which has now been replaced by housing. '7 union, workhouse, boys admitted' and later that year the school 'received payment from the Guardians of the poor.'

Speed 1964 [10], gives a chart taken from a school in Bath which indicates that Standard I started at age 8 and Standard VII contained 12 to 14 year olds. The range in each standard indicates that children did not move standards by age, as now but when they were ready for the next one. Examination by the inspectors would have shown their readiness, or not. In 1871, all over 7 are placed in standard II and II is then made into standard I, following the Elementary Education Act of 1870. A note is also made that entries in the log are to be made weekly according to the New Code. According to Quin [11], in 1876, 360 children aged 3 to 13 attended Manor, 213 went to the National, or Church School, 78 were going to Dame Schools, 83 were at private schools and 120 were not going anywhere.

There was a night school as well as day school, as there is a reference to 30 boys presenting for examination. One of the inspection reports comments that the rate of failure in the night school is much lower than in the day school.

Parents

Parents were to be elected as managers according to the trust deed and had to pay for their children's education. Absenteeism was rife, as schooling was not compulsory and often references are made as to the reasons for absence. I have included some of these in a separate section below. But one reference to parents during this time stands out because of its nature. Clearly parental temper is nothing new.

'Sent by her daughter an impertinent and threatening letter about PT, she further brought false charges against her and the Ass. Master and PTs. She also, because I kept her daughter in to examine the truth of the above, she entered school before dismissal causing a disturbance and although requested several times to leave she refused, compelling the master to put her out. In attempting to do so she viciously flung a stone which she had concealed in her hand at the master, fortunately missing him and struck him several times in the face with her clenched fist. Shortly after the master arrived at his house, an elder brother came to the house furiously throwing stones and dirt against the door.'

FIGURE 3.1 Revised Code of Standards 1862

STANDARD I	
READING	Narrative monosyllables
WRITING	Form on blackboard or slate. from dictation, letters capital and small manuscript.
ARITHMETIC	Form on blackboard or slate from dictation, figures up to 20, name at sight figures up to 20, add and subtract figures up to 10 orally from examples on the blackboard
STANDARD II	
READING	One of the narratives next in order after monosyllables in an elementary reading book used in the school
WRITING	Copy in manuscript character a line of print.
ARITHMETIC	A sum in simple addition or subtraction and the multiplication table.
STANDARD III	
READING	A short paragraph from a more advanced reading book.
WRITING	A sentence slowly dictated once by a few words at a time. from the same book.
ARITHMETIC	Long division and compound rules money.
STANDARD IV	
READING	A few lines of poetry or prose at the choice of the inspector.
WRITING	A sentence slowly dictated once by a few words at a time. from a reading book such as is used in the first class of the school.
ARITHMETIC	Compound rules common weights and measures.
STANDARD V	
READING	A short ordinary paragraph in a newspaper or other modern narrative.
WRITING	Another short ordinary paragraph in a newspaper or other modern narrative slowly dictated once by a few words at a time.
ARITHMETIC	Practice and bills of parcels.
STANDARD VI	
READING	To read with fluency and expression.
WRITING	A short theme or letter or an easy paraphrase.
ARITHMETIC	Proportion and fractions vulgar and decimal.

Curtis 1967, p 259

Fig. 3.1

Figure 3.2 Revised code of Standards 1872

STANDARD I	
READING	One of the narratives next in order after monosyllables in an elementary reading book used in the school.
WRITING	Copy in manuscript character a line of print and write from dictation a few common words.
ARITHMETIC	Simple addition and subtraction of numbers of not more than four figures and the multiplication table to multiplication by six.
STANDARD II	
READING	A short paragraph from an elementary reading book.
WRITING	A sentence from the same book slowly read once and then dictated in single words.
ARITHMETIC	The multiplication table and any simple rule as far as short division. inclusive.
STANDARD III	
READING	A short paragraph from a more advanced reading book.
WRITING	A sentence slowly dictated once by a few words at a time from the same book.
ARITHMETIC	Long division and compound rules money.
STANDARD IV	
READING	A few lines of poetry or prose at the choice of the inspector.
WRITING	A sentence slowly dictated once. by a few words at a time from a reading book such as is used in the first class of the school.
ARITHMETIC	Compound rules common weights and measures.
STANDARD V	
READING	A short ordinary paragraph in a newspaper. or other modern narrative.
WRITING	Another short ordinary paragraph in a newspaper. or other modern narrative. slowly dictated once by a few words at a time.
ARITHMETIC	Practice and bills of parcels.
STANDARD VI	
READING	To read with fluency and expression.
WRITING	A short theme or letter or an easy paraphrase.
ARITHMETIC	Proportion and fractions vulgar and decimal.

Fig. 3.2

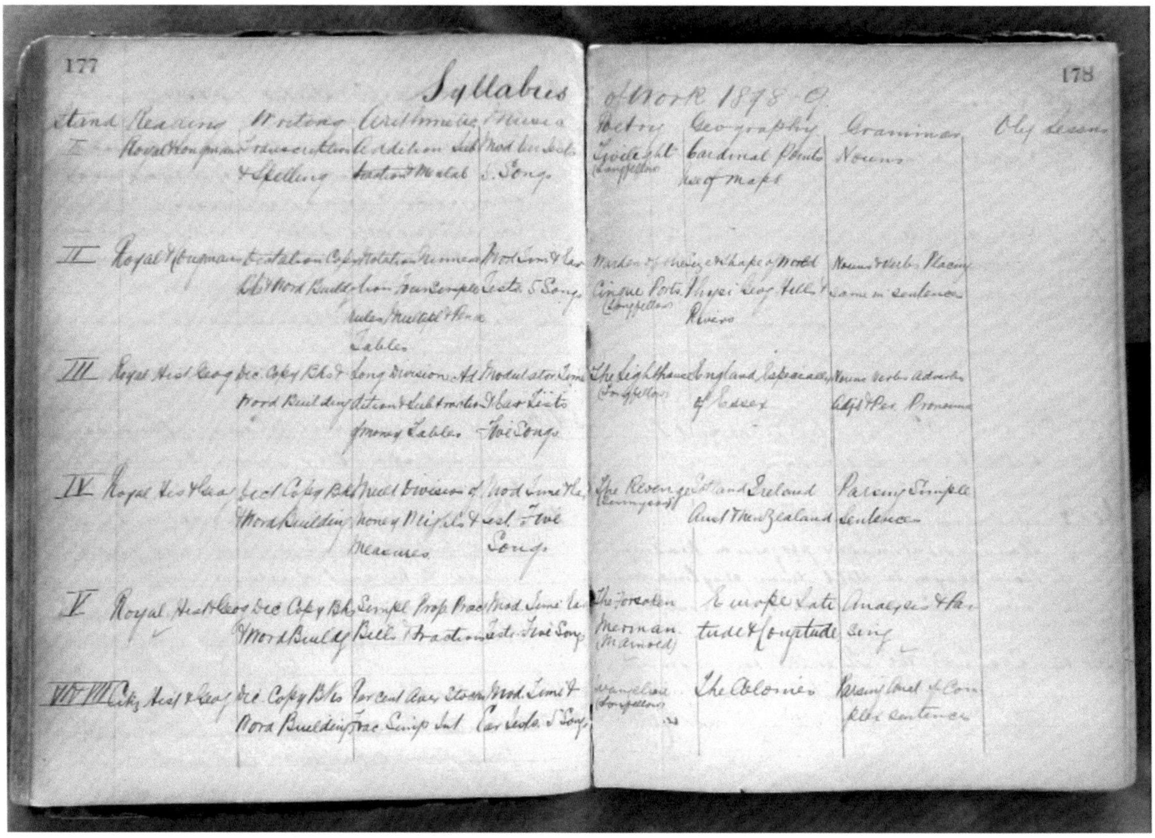

Photo 3.6 Syllabus for infants 1878-9 from log book.

It was not unknown in the 1870s for parents to withdraw children and send them to Dame Schools to prevent them being taught by girls.[12] Rowley also comments that in 1870 half the children in Essex were not receiving any education.

Teaching, Learning and Curriculum

What did they teach? The first entry in the main school junior log book was for June 1st 1863. It starts straight in with, 'Examined the fourth section in Reading, found their articulation of contracted words quite indistinct and timid. Ordered the monitors to dwell longer upon all words difficult to spell or pronounce.'

The payment by results, introduced in the Revised Code of 1862 continued to the 1890s. The Revised Code also introduced the standards to be reached by children which would be the basis for examination.[13] Fig. 3.1 & Fig 3.2

These got changed from time to time. For example, in 1872 the expectations of standards were as Fig 3.2.

Photo 3.6 shows how the standards were transcribed by the headteacher as a syllabus in the log book.

Some clues are given in the log books as to the content of lessons:

'Lesson to first section on numeration and another on chief parts of Europe.

Gallery lesson, The elephant.

List of songs given to inspector:

Oh, we can play on the big bass drum	See the little busy bee
Children go, to and fro	Holidays, Holidays
Come soft and lovely evening	Before the bright sun.'

Some of the material used for lessons seems rather adult by our standards.

'The children of the first section have just learnt, The Slave's Dream, by Longfellow, 8 verses and have today written it from memory.'

'Write from memory in dictation books the poem, The Village Blacksmith.'

'Drawing and singing lesson.'

'Went over four rules of decimals and gave some information on decimal coinage, to show importance of this to lads, ... audibly remarked he shouldn't want this. Hereafter, I made the opportunity for speaking on the importance of mental discipline for any and every calling.'

'Read from Arabian Nights in afternoon.'

'Macaulay's Horatius, for Home lessons.'

Seasonal material was also used, November 22nd in 1872 saw the children learning a New song, Ring out wild bells as well as Awake the starry midnight hour and King Christmas.

Equipment

In 1863 the head master indicates that 'he is changing the source of pencils, pens etc. and will supply them, at a halfpenny per month per scholar.' He later refers to slates being used and a blackboard.

Various primers are named from time to time and facsimiles of some can even be found by googling the names. For instance, the log books say:

'to copy from the manuscript characters in Laurie's First Standard reader. Laurie's reading sheets, for those who cannot manage first standard reading books, permission of the committee, prevents destruction of books, keeps a number of little children well employed.'

Copies of Laurie's readers in the Bodlean Library, Oxford, have been scanned to be available electronically.

'Mental Arithmetic employing McClollands book for examples.'

'Spelling from Mrs. Sewell's Dictation Exercises.'

'Davis' Spelling book used for columns of words for learning.'

Photo 3.7 Re-enactment of Victorian school room from 1987 pageant rehearsal.

Teaching and learning strategies

It is evident from the above there would have been a lot of rote learning. You only have to read in Dickens, "Hard Times" about Gradgrind's school. – 'Facts, what we need is facts' – to get a feel for the kind of teaching common in mid Victorian times. Mispronunciation is commented on and dictation, '2 mistakes, scholar in 13 lines.' This sounds rather like the sort of statistics that are gained from SATs standard assessment tasks .

Photo 3.8 Magic lantern in Wymondham Museum, Norfolk.

Children did not always seem to sit in desks but sat in rows on benches, sometimes in a gallery. If they were using slates, they must have balanced them on their knees. Photo 3.7

There was a lot of 3R learning but there are various clues in the log books of interesting activities and thought being given to ways of learning that show Manor as a school concerned with its pupils and their breadth of learning as well as the basics. Rearing of silkworms and making of things like papier maché are referred to in the infants. The heads were perceptive about teaching methods and what worked well for the children 'spelling is better or easier taught so as to allow the children to study their spellings at their desks from the reading lesson.' Allowing children to write things on their slates 'seems a quicker and more effective way of teaching names of rivers.'

Mr. Saunders tried out differing times of playtime to optimise the amount of work the children did in school and takes '7 of the dullest children to hear read at least once or twice daily with a view to find how much of their slow progress is attributable to the inattention of the monitors and how much to themselves.' He 'placed by themselves all children who commit errors in the copybooks or blot their books and allow them to return to the rest only after 6 copies have been written quite clear.' He adopted the method of reading the bible and occasionally giving the substance of one of the narrative alternately. 'The bare reading seems to attract only a minority of children.'

He sent newsletters home. He had a magic lantern show, candle powered, for the children at the end of the Christmas term, 1873 on Christmas eve. Photo 3.8

In 1876 Mr. Rose the then Master, 'took older scholars to London' presumably the Braintree railway close by offered easy access for such a trip. He later enters a very perceptive remark:

> 'Too much telling on teacher's part not enough educing, too much like preaching. Questioning poor.'

Behaviour issues

These seem to loom large in the early log books but as the recording of such issues was one of the purposes of the books, it is not surprising. Some of the entries again show a fairly enlightened approach and if we find it a bit barbarous in the 21st century to see records of the use of corporal punishment, at least the masters showed thoughtfulness in its application, with a care for standards of respect and general discipline. Early on, the master, Mr. Saunders, records even trying to do without corporal punishment .

> 'After a trial of 2 years strict non enforcement of never employing corporal punishment, it seems that some boys must occasionally see that a teacher has the right to enforce his commands, even with a stick.'

The heads record various misdemeanours:

> 'the seeming fondness of some of the bigger boys to strike the little ones.'

> 'instead of writing their words were running about the school.'

> 'unkind treatment to an old lady.'

> 'pulling girls about.'

> 'guilty of oaths and swearing at a girl with other gross language.'

The culprits were not always found as was the case with,

'some obscene words written on the wall outside.'
and with, 'little girl ... had her dinner taken by some scholar.'

It would have been a packed lunch. Not a lot seems to have changed.

Various rewards as well as punishments are tried out. 'Encouraging active boys by allowing them to leave school before the regular dismission a few minutes as a reward for quickly and correctly worked exercises' and 'the occasional distribution of a halfpenny I find acts as a capital incentive.'

The heads also gave pep talks to the pupils.

> 'The school is rather large and we have been obliged to address it collectively on points of order and behaviour such as the hanging up of bonnets, quietly closing doors, not speaking to teachers without permission, etc.'

> 'I spoke some ten minutes on the need of cultivating a kind and courteous treatment of each other. This comes from observing several ridiculing one whom they fancied not to be sufficiently clean in person. My aim was to show this was a cruel way to cure a fault and opposed to the golden rule.'

Attendance and social background

Attendance is also recorded, frequently along with various reasons. This was still the era of non compulsory schooling but non attendance meant a poor inspection result and thus less grant. Various external reasons are given.

> 'Heavy rains lower attendance.'

> 'Half day school only because of an agricultural show at Witham.'

> 'Annual cattle fair.'

> 'Fete day in Stistead.'

> 'Nomination of MPs for north Essex.'

> 'Excitement of election pending obliged to give half day's holiday.'

> 'There were only 29 scholars came to day being polling day. I therefore dismissed these.'

> 'entrance free of a hippodrome.'[14]

> 'gardens at Stistead Hall being thrown open.'

> 'Braintree May fair.'

> 'Scholars retained for gleaning.'

> 'Edmund's menagerie.'

> 'pea picking.'

56

Health Issues

This was a time before the age of antibiotics, surgery under anesthesia or a national health service. Children succumbed to illnesses nobody thinks about today. Jenner's use of cowpox vaccination in 1796 had proved efficacious and vaccination for smallpox became compulsory in Great Britain in the 1850s and the death rate from the disease fell markedly over the rest of the century. Yet it was still a feared disease as uptake of the vaccine was not immediately universal and epidemics still occurred in Braintree.

'Children absent in area where smallpox rages.'

'Dismissed 3 children 2 because their parents had smallpox in their houses.'

There were no vaccines for other viral diseases such as whooping cough and measles which still can also kill if the patient was already weak or the strain was severe. The recent MMR vaccine scare has brought a reduction in vaccinations and a recurrence of some serious cases of measles. Scarlet fever, also a potential killer was feared and its aetiology misunderstood. It is actually a rash due to a streptococcal sore throat infection and can easily be cured with antibiotics. It was feared even in the 1940s when it was still treated by isolation of the patient in a fever hospital and fumigation of the home. One wonders what disinfectant was used in the drains in 1881, probably carbolic acid. Lister was developing its use to provide antisepsis in surgery and the germ theory of Pasteur was becoming widely accepted by this time. Diseases like pneumonia and bronchitis were also potential killers because of lack of antibiotics.

'One Child died from abscess on the head.'

Simple boils could lead to septicemia when left untreated.

'Whooping cough.'

'Whooping cough and scarlet fever.'

'Measles.'

'Death from whooping cough and bronchitis.'

Scarlet fever, 'had all our drains and WCs flushed out with disinfectant and the schools sprinkled with the same.'

'Dismissed 1 girl for, being unclean.'

The entry possibly refers to headlice, a condition that is still a problem in schools today even though it is realized that clean children can be infested. Ordinarily, dirty children would have been fairly common as few of the poorer classes would have had piped water at this time, bathrooms were a luxury and hot water systems even more so.

Photo 3.9 Infant building enlarged from old print 1864.

One death is reported at length, an accident.

'Sad occurrence, fatal in five hours befell Shufflebotham. When dismissed from school, stopped short of playground to play with reversible roller. When deceased being on the frame behind, and though warned by ... , the others lifted shaft and being unable to hold it, the roller fell over and struck C.S. on the head.'

The next day the head, 'suggested to the children the desirability of showing the sympathy with poor C.S's parents by contributing towards his burial. All seemed willing to subscribe and the following day he records '180 subscribed from 2s. to ½d, sum total, £2.5s.2½ which I handed over to Mr. S. with a letter of condolence. He was overcome with a feeling of gratitude. He received from us in all over £3.'

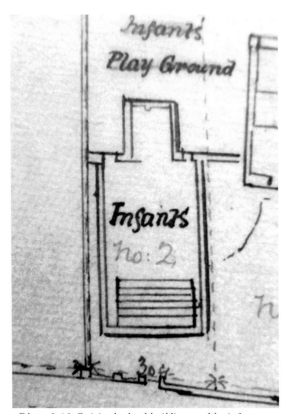

Photo 3.10 Original school building used by infants, as seen on 1895 deeds.

The building and local environment

The infant school was a separate physical entity. The 1864 sketch shown in the first chapter. Photo 1.1 , also shows the building to the west of the main building. Photo 3.9

The plan drawn on the 1895 deeds when the school was handed over to the local school board even shows the gallery. Photo 3.10

The early reference in the deeds to a possible future master's house, common in many rural schools still, was never built.

The overwhelming impression given by that opening ceremony described in the last chapter is one of a glorious purpose built school but the log book records show that all is not well even from fairly early times .

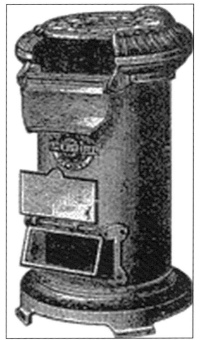

Photo 3.11 Tortoise stove.

In 1877 it is recorded that 'The great nuisance to the school is the insufficiency of ventilation, the downdraft so great, compelled to close them, poisonous atmosphere.' The inspection report of that date mentions the 'defection of ventilation' but also 'the absence of any classroom of sufficient size, useless platform at end of room and absence of soap and towels in lavatories.'

A 'sickening smell of gas' is reported in December 1879 and finally in the summer of 1881, 'part of the ceiling under belfry fell down being rotten from damp.' This 1862 building was already a building with problems. In 1866, 'One family left owing to heat of room exposing children to colds.' Hot water pipes were mentioned in the description of the building referred to in the last chapter and later certainly there were coke fired boilers to be found underground at the rear of the school. Anyone who has dealing with coke fired things knows that fumes can be a problem. The room at the back of the building had a fireplace and this was presumably the heating for that room. This may have been used as the master's room or a classroom.

It seems there was some kind of heating in the infant building, possibly from what are sometimes called tortoise stoves. The author had such a one in the village school in Suffolk where she started teaching in the early 1970s, it was a free standing stove with a chimney going directly up through the roof, coke fired and refuelled by the caretaker every lunchtime. It was too hot for the children to sit near in the winter. Photo 3.11

An inspection report in 1880 records:

'On the whole this is the very worst Infant School I have inspected for a long time. The walls of the new classroom were dripping with wet and totally unfit for the use of young children.'

The log book later comments that, 'the Room is still too dark in dull weather and the ventilation's not good especially in the new part.'

The next month the comment reads, 'Wall of classroom appears damper today than I have before noticed them although a good fire has been kept.'

Inspectors suggested a lobby or porch as a cloakroom for outdoor clothes for the infants in January of 1877 and some kind of new room is 'used for first time in 1880.'

Lighting was by gas from fairly early on and that also could have added to the fumes. Even with this installation, it is only five years later that there is a recommendation to improve the lighting. Windows were difficult to operate for ventilation. They were and are still high and caused draughts when opened. The infant mistress 'wrote to Mr. Brown of Crittall and Brown, on state of windows casement in gallery through opening windows in dinner hour without permission.'

These were buildings with problems.

END NOTES

[1] Gosden, 1989

[2] 9th February 1876 J

[3] Quin, 1981

[4] Speed, 1964

[5] Silver and Silver, 1974 p.74

[6] Silver and Silver. 1974

[7] Silver and Silver, 1974

[8] Murry N. 1996 p 193

[9] Murry N. 1996 p.339

[10] Speed 1964

[11] Quin, 1981

[12] Rowley, 1974

[13] Curtis,1967 p. 259

[14] a hippodrome appears to be the combination of a music hall and a circus. Google

Chapter 4 The headship of Mr. Davies 1882–1913

Background and context

This era of headship also coincides with an era of British history covering twenty years of the nineteenth century the end of the lengthy Victorian era and the years that led up to the first World War, WW1. During this time also, photography became much more widespread and we are able to actually see the staff and children who worked at the school from photographs. The period covers two changes of monarch and many changes of social attitude. The log books refer only briefly to what must have been quite momentous occasions. No mention is made of Victoria's death but there was a

'Distribution of medals and tickets for the coronation to be held tomorrow.'

Edward VII's death and George V's coronation get a little more attention.

'The funeral of the late king having been arranged for Friday 20th Monday and Tuesday of same week will be Whit closure, school closed all week.'

'Broke up on Friday afternoon for Coronation week.'

'1 week's holiday for coronation.'

Mr. Smith's letter sent to the school on the occasion of the 125th anniversary detailed many memories of his time at school. He tells us that he remembered "the funeral of King Edward VII and the coronation of King George V and Queen Mary and the atmosphere of carnivalism with the whole school and most of Braintree. Children were marched down London Road to Lyndon Meadow where we were given a tea, a bag of sweets and a coronation mug with King George V and Queen Mary upon it. Everybody walking pushing their exhibits on barrow or horse and cart as there was very little motorised transport about during that time of day. We had to assemble in the long room in the infants school."[1]

The turn of the century was a time of national confidence and general prosperity following some depression in the 1880s. The infant head had a 'letter from the Board refusing an increase of salary because of the general depression and the greater outlet to be met by the board.'

There was however also an increasing awareness of inequalities between people, particularly in gender and class. Despite the effect of the death of Victoria and the Boer War on morale,

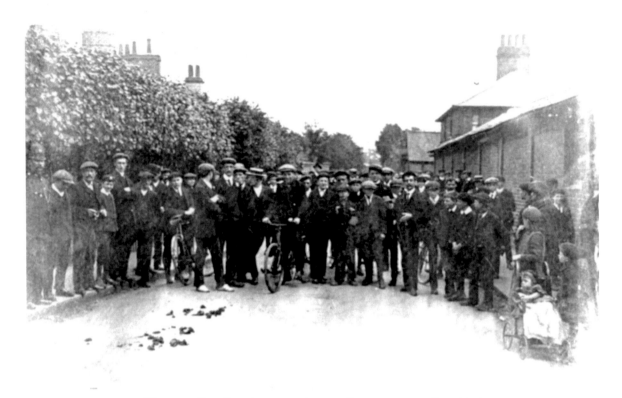

Photo 4.1 Crittall workers on strike over efficiency measures, June 1912

Britain celebrated its belief in being a great nation on 24th May 1902. It saw itself as the owner of an empire which spanned the world. Schools, including Manor, joined in what became an annual event. 'The school flag hoisted for the first time on Mon. morning May 25th at 11 am in commemoration of Empire Day 1908.'

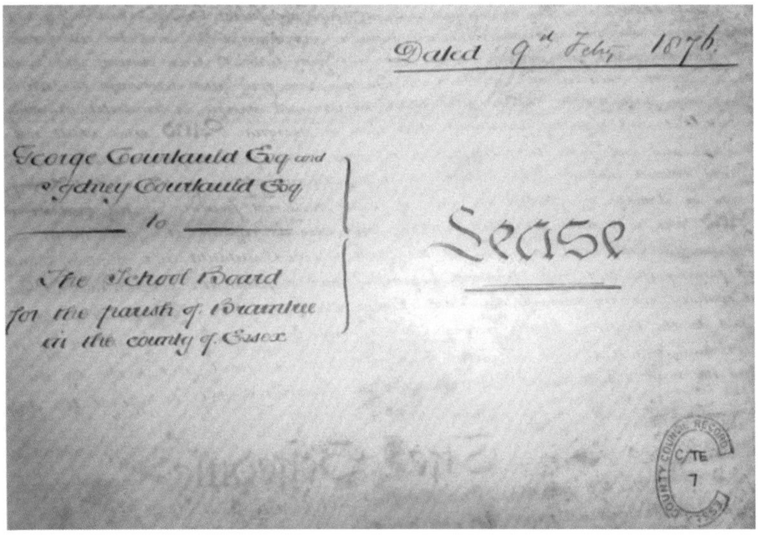

Dated 9th Feby 1876.

George Courtauld Esq and Sydney Courtauld Esq

to

The School Board for the parish of Braintree in the county of Essex

Lease

C/TE 7

Photo 4.2 Lease of school by trustees to Braintree Board 1876

This was a period in which Braintree was thriving. Crittall's opened their factory at the far end of Manor Street in 1893 having started manufacturing its famous metal windows in 1884. Lake began his bicycle business in

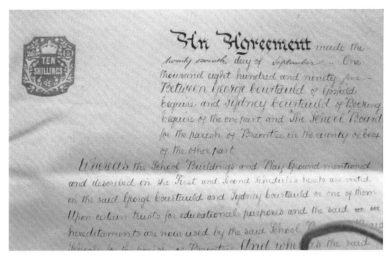

Photo 4.3 Deed of transfer of ownership 1895

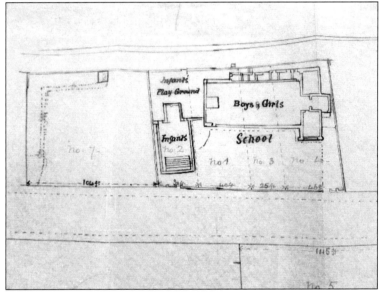

Photo 4.4 Separate sheet attached to 1895 deed with plan showing main building and old infant school layouts

1892 and with Elliot produced motorcycles from 1904–5, the firm later becoming a well known manufacturer of car, aircraft and tank parts. Warner's moved in to take over the silk weaving buildings in South Street in 1895.

The education history books describe the building of many schools at busy junctions which have problems with noise and smells as well as suffering all the internal problems that were remarked about Manor Street School. The market always spilled over from the market place to outside the school windows and in the late Victorian times the cattle market was also close by. The noise and smell from this must have been awful. Certainly, noise from the market was a problem up to the time the school closed. Gardner [2] in his chapter on teachers, suggests that while people may look to the changes in the law or political ambition, actually the main constraints for teachers are their individual circumstances – the pressures of minimal space or insufficient resources or equipment.

During this time education had become universal, compulsory and free. The 1876 act had made it compulsory for parents to see that their children were adequately educated in the 3 Rs; they could be fined if they did not do it. By 1891 parents were given the right to demand free education; the school leaving age was raised to 11 and 12 in 1899. Local school boards were set up and the Braintree and Bocking of which one was to administer the Manor Street schools, Infant and Junior and the four schools of Bocking. George and Sydney Courtauld leased the Manor Street Schools to the new board in 1876 and 'the board decided to accept

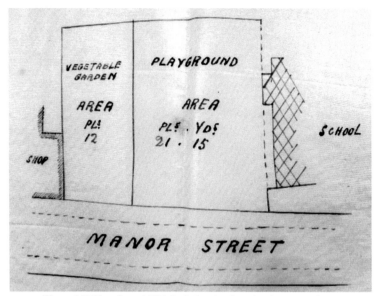

Photo 4.5 Plan from 1897 deed showing how lot 7 was made up

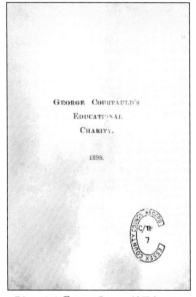

Photo 4.6 George Courtauld Education Charity foundation booklet cover

the fee grant from Sept 1st 1891 and no charges are to be made for any school materials for the children between 3 and 15 years.' Photo 4.2

Governance

The archives held in the ERO and the museum have deeds and abstracts of the earlier deeds dated 1895 covering the final handover of the trustees to the Braintree and Bocking School Board. Photo 4.3 & 4.4

On 27th September 1895 George and Sidney Courtauld:

• conveyed to the school board all their interest without restriction, all the school buildings and playground and the £1,000 endowment

• sold and the school board purchased, all items mentioned in the third schedule being the real estate of the endowment

• conveyed the abstracts of the title deeds

• made application to the Charity Commissioners for the establishment of a scheme for the future administration of the endowment fund to give exhibitions for scholars attending schools, to be called exhibitions, to be tenable at any university or place of higher education awarded from time to time by the Board or a competent person at their request

• undertook all costs of conveyancing these items to the school board, this being the School board of the parish of Braintree .

The trustees were only George and Sydney Courtauld by that time. Edward Craig was released from being a trustee in 1867. Thomas Challis had died. David Rees had left Braintree before the opening of the 1861 building. An 1871 document grants indemnity to any other Courtauld family members named in the older George Courtauld's will from any further responsibility towards the school. An 1897 conveyance transfers the ownership of a piece of

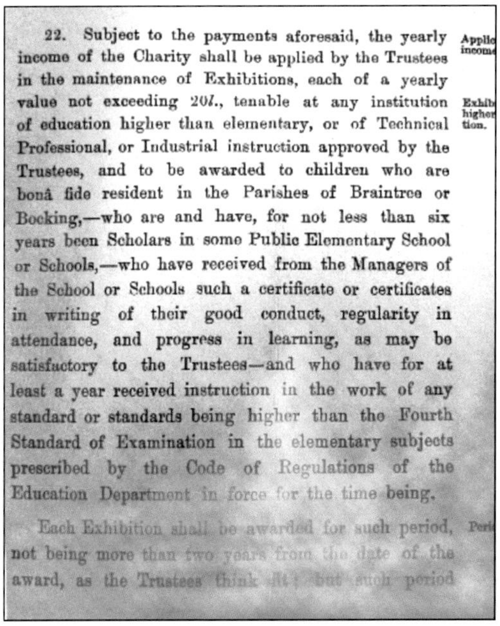

22. Subject to the payments aforesaid, the yearly income of the Charity shall be applied by the Trustees in the maintenance of Exhibitions, each of a yearly value not exceeding 20*l.*, tenable at any institution of education higher than elementary, or of Technical Professional, or Industrial instruction approved by the Trustees, and to be awarded to children who are bonâ fide resident in the Parishes of Braintree or Bocking,—who are and have, for not less than six years been Scholars in some Public Elementary School or Schools,—who have received from the Managers of the School or Schools such a certificate or certificates in writing of their good conduct, regularity in attendance, and progress in learning, as may be satisfactory to the Trustees—and who have for at least a year received instruction in the work of any standard or standards being higher than the Fourth Standard of Examination in the elementary subjects prescribed by the Code of Regulations of the Education Department in force for the time being.

Each Exhibition shall be awarded for such period, not being more than two years from the date of the award, as the Trustees think fit : but such period

Photo 4.7 A page from George Courtauld Education Charity foundation booklet

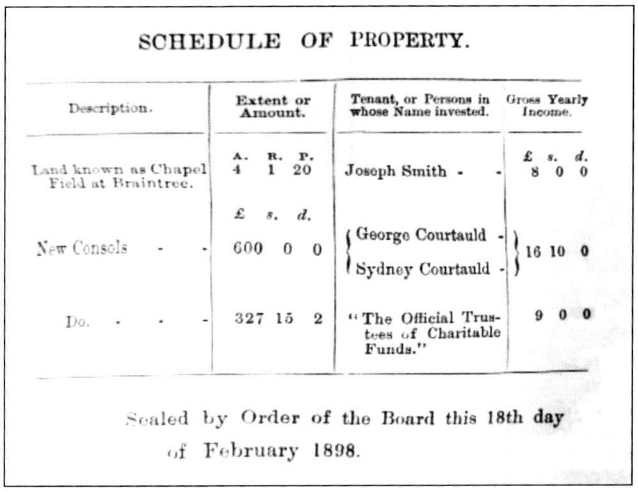

SCHEDULE OF PROPERTY.

Description.	Extent or Amount.	Tenant, or Persons in whose Name invested.	Gross Yearly Income.
Land known as Chapel Field at Braintree.	A. R. P. 4 1 20	Joseph Smith	£ s. d. 8 0 0
New Consols	£ s. d. 600 0 0	George Courtauld Sydney Courtauld	16 10 0
Do.	327 15 2	"The Official Trustees of Charitable Funds."	9 0 0

Sealed by Order of the Board this 18th day of February 1898.

Photo 4.8 Page showing purchase of Chapel Hill Field from George Courtauld Education Charity foundation booklet.

land to the west of the two school buildings to the board, this was to enable the new infant school to be built on it. Photo 4.5

At the same time, the endowment fund, originally £1,000, was transferred to set up the George Courtauld Educational Charity in 1898. There is a small booklet describing the full details of the Courtauld endowment fund and its administration in the museum. Sydney was offered a place on the board but refused.[3] The Courtauld family had retained an interest for many years after the opening, they often visited the school and signed the registers. The 'School treat' was held 'in Mr. Courtauld's grounds 1890.' Even after the transfer 'Miss Courtauld has kindly presented an attendance banner to the school and there is keen competition for its possession by all the classes.'

It is quite clear the proceeds of the endowment were not to be used for poor relief but for those entering higher education. One entry in the log books of this time refers to the award but with no details. There are also references in the manager's minutes where they indicate that an examination was necessary to gain the award. There are two packs in the ERO of the details of beneficiaries and correspondence from 1905, 1909 and 1922–1945. Cunnington's, solicitors in Braintree still administer a George Courtauld Educational Charity.[4] One of the purchases with the endowment money had been Chapel Hill Field. See Photo 1.6 and Photo 4.8

It took until the turn of the century to really put together any cohesive vision of what sort of education was wanted in England. The major act of 1902 [5] did away with school boards and empowered local education authorities, LEAs to run elementary, secondary and technical schools. Board schools became council schools, if the LEA provided the buildings and voluntary, if they did not. LEA schools would be supported by local rates, with the government providing grants for poorer districts, rather than the grants going directly to schools depending on the results of their inspections.

Schools were to have a board of 6 managers, their constitution varying with the foundation. Manor became a council 'provided' school as the buildings and land had already been handed over to the local board. Instruction was determined by the LEA who would decide on the number and qualifications of the teachers and could also dismiss teachers. Religious instruction would be undenominational, which had been the case at Manor since its inception. Managers' later Governors' minutes for the school date from 1903 until the school closed and are all in the ERO. Until certainly the 1960s, the managers met to discuss all the Braintree and Bocking council schools together at each meeting, just like the original board.

People

Managers post 1903

From the minutes available in the ERO, the managers appear to be micro managing the school leaving the heads with few responsibilities except for day to day matters. They met every fortnight visiting the schools in their care in between. They covered:

- hiring and monitoring of teacher competence,
- small items of repair, all expenditure on equipment and furniture,
- insurance,
- the syllabus, even considering hymns,
- arrangement of playtimes,
- Courtauld scholarships approved after examinations,
- all requisitions for stationery etc. which had to be approved by managers after their visits.

Headteacher

This was for Manor a time of stability. One headteacher alone was head of the junior school, Mr R.N. Davies. He sadly died just before the First World

Photo 4.9 Infant school staff outside their new building 1897

66

War after an unsuccessful operation. 'Mr. Davies, headmaster, absent to undergo an operation at University College Hospital London' 'News received of death of Mr. Davies.'

Teachers

Because of the interest in education for all there was also a greatly increased emphasis on the training of teachers but the monitorial system still seems to have been in existence up to the turn of the century.

'Several teachers from other towns visited the school this week.'

'Mistress left school at 3.45pm in order to attend a meeting held at the Mechanics Institute in reference to forming central classes for pupil teachers.'

'J.M.B. absent from morning lessons on Monday morning. I had taken no notice of her absence the previous week as it was that succeeding her scholarship examination in London. I asked her to account for her absence and her reply was her mother told her to stop at home for a fortnight. Of course, this is a direct violation of her indentures.'

'Both teachers and monitors attend evening classes on Monday evenings at the school room.'

It must have been hard for someone who had possibly left their own schooling at 13 or 14 to begin a college course at 18, hence presumably the continuing existence of monitors. Photo 4.9 shows the infant teachers outside their new building. The managers' minutes sometimes give names of the teachers with their training status, they were not all certificated.

Elementary schools made up the bulk of schools and 76 per cent of the teaching staff were women.[6] Generally, these women would make teaching a lifelong career, although they would have had to resign their posts if they got married. To qualify as a teacher they were expected to study at university level in addition to doing practical training for three years, largely non residential. There were only four universities in 1900, training would have been at a provincial college. While universities rarely accepted women, the colleges did. Secondary school teachers were considered qualified to teach merely by having a degree in the subject. By the 1890s, pupil teacher evening classes were possible and grants towards training were made available. Teacher training regulations were established in 1904 and 1907. The first Essex training college opened in Saffron Walden in 1884 but there was no pupil teacher centre in the county until the 1890s.[7]

In 1904 'Pupil teachers commenced going to the Chelmsford Centre this week.'

Photo 4.10 Younger children 1895 – 1910

Photo 4.11 Class VII 1895 – 1910

Photo 4.12 Older children 1890– 1910

Photo 4.13 Older children 1890– 1910

Children

Some concern was voiced in the log books about standards.

> In 1886 the head 'Admitted 2 or 3 children lately 5 years of age who do not know 3 letters of alphabet. Can neither write from the very simplest copy nor do anything else. I was obliged to place such children with the three year olds.' There is little about any sort of extra support for those who fell behind. They just had to stay down and repeat a year. 'Std one is not making satisfactory progress in reading. especially the children from the workhouse.'
>
> 'Rearranged classes this week. Examined Std 1 just sent up from the infant dept. and find reading much below the standard of last year. In fact 16 out of the fifty seven do not know the alphabet.'

Social conditions were held responsible for slowness or a child was 'defective.' The earliest attempt to help children with special needs as they are now called, was in the 1899 Education Defective and Epileptic Children Act. This empowered school boards to provide special accommodation but it was not made obligatory until 1914. Prior to this a few pioneers had opened their own schools to support such children, Bradford authority being one in 1894. Children were categorised in a hierarchy, not by their needs but by a diagnosis of their condition. Children were labelled and teachers and schools were set up to deal with these types. The 1913 Mental Deficiency Act, with the 1914 addition about their education, named four main groups: idiots, imbeciles, feeble minded and moral imbeciles. These latter could be bright children who were, for instance, thieves.

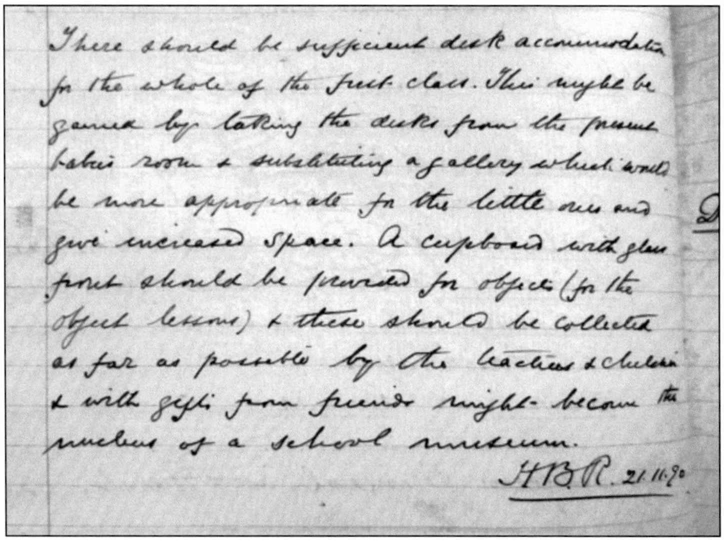
There should be sufficient desk accommodation for the whole of the first class. This might be gained by taking the desks from the present babies room & substituting a gallery which would be more appropriate for the little ones and give increased space. A cupboard with glass front should be provided for objects (for the object lessons) & these should be collected as far as possible by the teachers & children & with gifts from friends might become the nucleus of a school museum.

HBR. 21.11.90

Photo 4.14 An infant school inspection report in log book 1890

Some concern was raised over social conditions by the headteachers with comments like 'Several children came to school with dirty boots this morning.' 'The number of children who claim exemption so as to go to work is largely increasing.' Elementary schools took children until they were 14, when they could leave and go out to work, although some left earlier. '5 children all over 12 examined and passed for Labour certificates.'

The photographs from the period show a variety of clothing some of which could be indicative of their family's financial condition. There were no uniforms. All the children however are shod. The oldest children are clearly of what we would now call secondary age, in their early teens. It is a bit amusing to see the women teachers wearing hats although it may only have been for the photographs. Photos 4.10, 4.11, 4.12 & 4.13

One entry is rather nice:

> 'Chairman and other managers were present at the school on Friday afternoon for the purpose of presenting Mabel Ludgater with a certificate from the Royal Humane Society for rescuing a little girl from drowning in the river Blackwater.'

Parents.

The role of parents was increasingly recognised as important but as ever their involvement could be seen as a mixed blessing as several entries describe.

> 'Parents complaining of children out of control, beyond parental authority, openly defy commands. Another came yesterday imploring me to chastise their children for disobedience.'

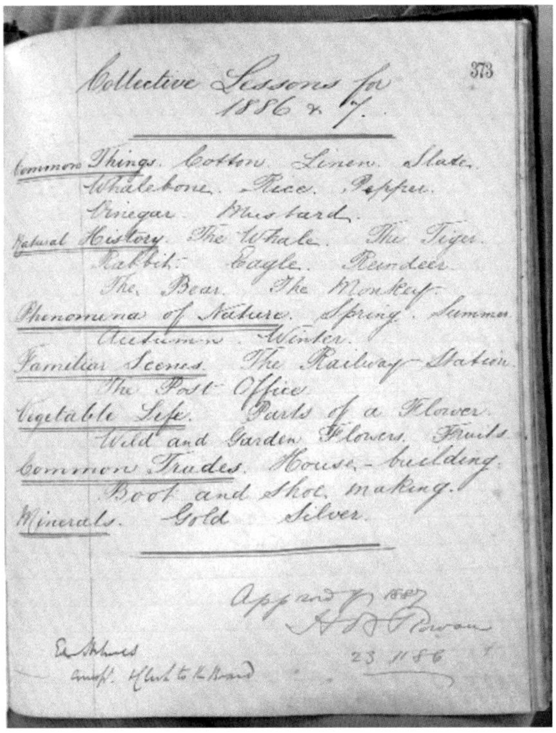

373

Collective Lessons for
1886 & 7.

Common Things. Cotton. Linen. Slate.
Whalebone. Rice. Pepper.
Vinegar. Mustard.
Natural History. The Whale. The Tiger.
Rabbit. Eagle. Reindeer.
The Bear. The Monkey.
Phenomena of Nature. Spring. Summer.
Autumn. Winter.
Familiar Scenes. The Railway Station.
The Post Office.
Vegetable Life. Parts of a Flower.
Wild and Garden Flowers. Fruits.
Common Trades. House-building.
Boot and Shoe making.
Minerals. Gold Silver.

Approved 1887
23 11 86

Photo 4.15 Infant scheme of work from log book 1886.

> 'I ... of Manor Street wish my son to be exempt from homework.'

> 'Punished a boy this week by giving him one stripe on the hand for fighting in school after having been warned twice previously for the same offence. Both parents came into school about it, the father in a heat of passion and made a great noise.' [entry here crossed out and initialled by the Board secretary] 'Some parents are under the impression they can walk into school as if it were their own house and threaten any teacher with the board as if the board existed only for their own grievance.'

There were even open days with parents invited to observe their children at work.

> 'Most of the children's parents visited the school having had notes of invitation yesterday, saw the kindergarten work and saw the children sing, drill.'

Competition between schools existed.

'One parent thinks of removing her two boys from these to the church schools because they receive prizes there.' and, 'a new boy came from the church school this morning and Miss Hemming sent him home with my knowledge and permission as he came to her to avoid punishment for impudence.'

Teaching, Learning and the Curriculum

The revised code of 1890 abolished the grant for the 3Rs, raised the fixed grant and retained a grant for classes and specific subjects but schools were still inspected. Photo 4.14

More subjects were added from 1893 to 1896 and 1897 saw the end of payment by results. This freed schools from the rigid testing and inspection regime. Encouragement was given to plan class visits to museums and art galleries.

'The teachers must in future test the work of their classes monthly and enter the results in their record book to be followed by a quarterly examination by myself.'

'Whole scheme of work for school will have to be recast for the new requirements of the code, a considerable amount of new apparatus will be required.'

This freedom from testing was short lived, being replaced by the introduction of the Free Place examination in 1907, causing schools to vie with one another in competing for the scholarships. A school's reputation became dependent on how many passed the examination. Children were coached for the examination in the three Rs and intelligence. Binet and Simon had developed the first scale of problems supposedly measuring intelligence or intellectual competence in 1905.

Photo 4.16 Ball frame or abacus in museum.

Children could then be categorised by mental age. Verbal reasoning, sometimes called intelligence tests, are still used to select children for grammar schools in the 11+ examination. It is well known that the scores in these tests can be improved with practice.

The new set of regulations published in 1904 said that the purpose of elementary school was to fit children practically and intellectually to the work of life, to help them reach their potential and become upright and useful members of the community. These were much broader aims than the previous standards set for Payment by results .

> 'Some readjustment in the order of teaching in arithmetic and Geography and a little more freedom in the periodical tests might not improbably be useful.'

1905 also saw the publication of "Suggestions for the consideration of teachers and others concerned in the work of Public Elementary Schools." Both of these included a recognition of the needs of the child, the beginnings of a child centred view of education by the establishment.[8]

Mr. Smith tells us that he started school in 1910, aged 4½, where he soon settled down to counting beads and playing with beads and wooden blocks with pictures on them. "In the next class we were taught the letters of the alphabet and how to pronounce them and we were taught to write upon a slate and count beads with a large bead frame and we began to get the foundation of learning the three Rs".[9] Photo 4.16

READING – was taught largely with primers, for instance, 'The Holborn.' The infant head comments when introducing 'the graphic infant primer in the first class, the children are greatly interested in the coloured illustrations.' It is not clear whether the letters were learnt by sounds or their names, possibly both. 'In the Babies and 3rd class, each child has a card suspended from its neck containing a capital letter on one side, a small letter on the other. By this means I am having word building taught. The children are very much interested and more eager to learn the letters.'

It is not clear whether juniors had primers or books of a wider interest. There were 'several reading books lying about the school.' The first public library had opened in 1848 but it was a very slow growing movement. The first free one opened in Leeds in 1877. Braintree library staff were unable to tell me when the first library opened in Braintree.

WRITING – was still done on slates according to Mr. Smith right up to the WW1, certainly in the infants. The log book entries for this period give us a good idea of how they were actually used and reused, with their wet rubbers. The references were all for the infants. The head 'ordered two dozen open porcelain wells for desks in order that the children may have water with which to clean their slates. Mrs. Courtauld has kindly offered to provide rubbers.' 'Part of the water wells arrived and fixed in desks, holes made in desks to hold same.' 'I have today received one shilling's worth of cloth for slate rubbers in order that every child may be supplied one.'

The slates were not plain, the head 'had 3 doz. Kindergarten Drawing slates repainted as the red lines could not be seen clearly by the children.'

Sand trays were also used to introduce letters and later 'the second class are also improving in writing on paper with lead pencils.'

Photo 4.17 Memorabilia brought in for 125ᵗʰ anniversary exhibition

ARITHMETIC – which had been a largely rote activity, was changing. There is a comment about 'a good deal of UNNECESSARY NOISE BEING CREATED by some of the classes saying tables aloud.' However, an inspector's report suggests that 'the curriculum of the lower classes might be improved by the introduction of more concrete work in arithmetic.' A ball frame, such as the museum still has, is mentioned in one report. Photo 4.16

PRACTICAL WORK – was also increasing as there was more recognition of the vocational role schools had to play. The head actually went to 'Stockholm to undergo a course of instruction in woods at the request of Essex County Council.' By 1910, there are mentions of technical instruction, handicraft training and cookery lessons. It must be remembered that children stayed at Manor for all their schooling, until they were 13 or 14.

Photo 4.18 Children rehearsing Swedish Drill for 1987 pageant

Pestalozzi in the late 18th century had inspired Froebel in the mid 19th century with more exploratory styles of education but English people did not like ideas coming in from other countries and those who did, thought such freer methods were only for the youngest children. Froebel and later Montessori emphasised the importance of activity, exploration and play. Rousseau in the late 18th century had ideas about developmental stages of children's understanding but this was not well understood in Britain. Dewey, more generally known for his work on library systems of classification, also promoted hands on learning at this time, reconstructing a form of Froebel's teaching in the early years of the 20th century. This did not seem to influence teaching at Manor very much. There is a little reference to paper mat making, plaiting and needle drill in the infants but after 7 years old more formal methods were still to be used. The revised code had hampered any general development of the curriculum and change was slow to percolate the system. Some of the needlework done in this period was brought in for the 125th anniversary celebrations but we do not know who by. One of the infant teachers was a Miss Beth Fenton. Annie may have been a relative. The stitching on the small garments had to be seen to be believed, it was so small. Photo 4.17

SCIENCE – was becoming a bit more practical. Object lessons had become another example of repeating facts but had been a move on from chalk and talk. A Professor Armstrong's heuristic method[10] was against the rote learning and wanted progressive discovery involving observation, experiment and use of inference. While this sounded the death knell of the object lesson and encouraged much more practical work, he was not very conversant with child development and appropriate work for different ages was not well planned. Again the infants seemed to have more interesting things going on. 'The children are taking a great interest in some silkworms being reared at school and are frequently allowed to see them and chat with the teacher about them.' This extract seems advanced for the time in allowing the children to chat with the teacher.

MUSIC – still seems to have been largely singing, with the occasional record appearing of some rather patriotic and adult songs.

'1886 Poetry I The field mouse. Chamber's Rdr Pg 87

    II Birds nest. New Holborn Rdr Pg 95

    III Health. Eliza Cook 306 Pg

    IV May queen. Defence of Lucknow by Tennyson crossed out.

    V–VII Continuation of Merchant of Venice

  Songs. 1 Come join with me 2. Now pray me for our country

    3. Onward into battle   4. Boat song

    5. Come let us make our voices ring.'

PHYSICAL EDUCATION, – as distinct from active learning of a subject however was well into the curriculum at this time. The increasing interest in physical health had put an

Photo 4.19 Foundation stone of Infant building

emphasis on physical development through games and exercises. Marching was sometimes taught by military personnel as a result of its inclusion in the 1871 Code. Swedish drill was introduced into London schools in 1879 and schools introduced a musical element to assist the classes. The head of the infant school asked for a harmonium, 'in order to teach the children musical drill.' She received it two years later but it disappeared. Later the head records, 'I have had the floor lined with red and blue paint for musical drill and marching.'

Presumably the infants were in the new building by then. '1st, 2nd classes are learning Swedish drill.' Later, 'Tambourine drill taken on Wednesday the girls wearing jackets. the boys scarves.' There are few records of physical activity in the junior school. Maybe the harmonium taken from the infant department and was used for musical drill in the juniors. In the juniors 'The inspector suggested that piano should be purchased for the older scholars in their Swedish drill exercises.' The photo 4.18 shows children practising Swedish drill for the 1987 pageant.

The infant log book records 'Maypole exercises' and Mr. Smith confirms its use with its coloured ribbons "around which we had to dance".[11]

By 1895 most towns had a school organisation for the promotion of football thanks to the South London Schools Football association formed in 1885 for elementary schools in that area. Matches between areas developed. Manor was always hampered by lack of its own playing field. Some schools tried cricket and others swimming. Athletics and rugby also became popular. The managers suggested trying to hire part of Fairfield for organised games in 1906 and put in a request to Braintree Urban District Council but it did not seem to materialise.

It was not all hard work. Children were given half holidays for 'children's entertainment in the evening. Have sold a good number of tickets, on account of the opening of the public gardens this afternoon.'

Discipline

Punishments in some cases appear harsh by our standards especially as corporal punishment was used. Other punishments seem to fit the crime and show imagination, or common sense. Certainly the things that get punished seem very familiar .

For example:

'big girls about chalking on the playground walls'

'two little boys took two inkwells'

'boy for kicking his teacher'

'boy for using bad language in the playground'

'two boys for unmercifully snowballing the girls and foot passengers'

'boy broke a pane of glass in the girl's lobby'

'truanting, one or two incorrigible young thieves'

'climbing on the wall in the playground'

'girls remain to gossip'

'boys, remaining at the back of the school instead of going into the playground'

'boys have taken to truanting in order to go to the golf ground to carry the members clubs.' 'this evil is on the increase'

Parents were involved and sometimes the police, the latter, 'particularly with respect to a boy R... .' A truanting boy was 'caned. I gave him one strike on each hand and detained him half an hour after school sending a note to his mother. Mrs ... afterwards called to see me about the matter and said she had whipped him and put him to bed for the rest of the day.'

'The school of late has been constantly visited by policemen.'

Teachers could also be disciplined. Miss B seemed to have a problem. In 1884 'her books and slates were again all over the school. I have to be constantly reminding her of these things.' Then later the junior head 'Spoke to Miss B this morning about slapping a child on the head. I have noticed this going on for sometime. When told of it asked what she was to do with them as children were sent out for punishment and no notice was taken of them. She spoke in a very impertinent manner to me and ended up saying. "I don't care, they can do as they like." This is not the first time this teacher has been rude to me.'

Timing and attendance or lack of it

Despite the legal requirement for attendance at school, it was clearly a problem in the late nineteenth century. Little children were still being admitted in the nineteenth century 'some of these are under three years.' In 1888, the infant head 'gave a slate pencil to each child who had made 10 attendances this week. Only 35 of 136 having accomplished this.' In 1898, she records '200 names on books 160 present.'

However things seemed to have improved by 1910 and the junior head grants 'a holiday because attendance above 92 for month.'

Sometimes. the children just took themselves off for fun. 'A very poor attendance Friday afternoon through circus admitting children free of charge to afternoon performance.'

Sometimes though, they were needed for essential harvesting activities 'gathering. blackberries.' 'more for pea picking than gleaning.'

Health Issues

The period at the beginning of the twentieth century not only saw a more liberal approach to the curriculum in its concern for the child as well as the subject matter but it also saw in

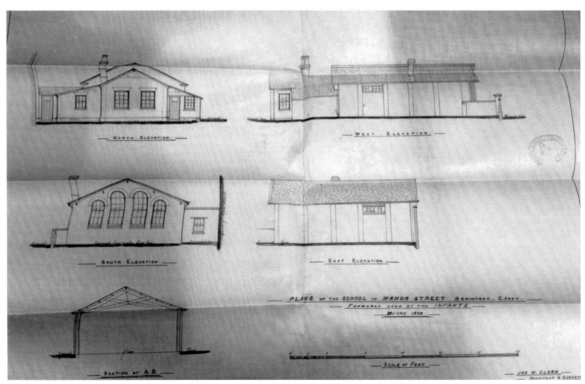

Photo 4.20 Drawings of old infant building done by Mr. Clark

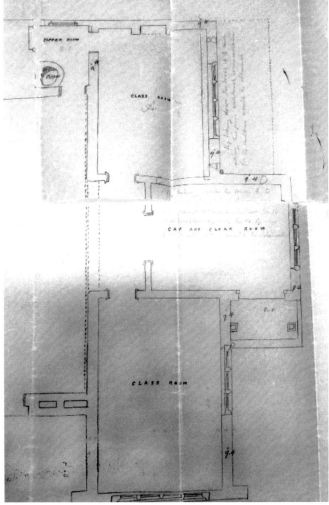

Photo 4.21 Builder's sketch of old infant school's extensions with more suggestions for creating space

1906 and 1907 the introduction of the school meals service and the school medical service. Medical inspections had started in London in 1890 and were certainly established in Braintree by 1912. What is more, a lady doctor 'visited the school for medical examinations.'

Measles and mumps along with scarlet fever and whooping cough were still important, measles being a killer and influenza was a problem. The distinction between viruses and bacteria was not yet made and sulphur was used as a disinfectant.

Scarlet fever closed one or other of the schools in 1890, 1894, 1896 and 1899 .

Measles did the same in 1886, 1887, 1891, 1896 and 1904.

Whooping cough, mumps, and influenza are also mentioned.

Antibiotics were still undiscovered. Eczema was still thought to be contagious so children were 'partially isolated as they were suffering eczema.' Ringworm was also a problem.

Buildings and Furniture

Heating, ventilation and overcrowding issues still seem to concern the writers of the log books and the inspectors, particularly in the old infant building .

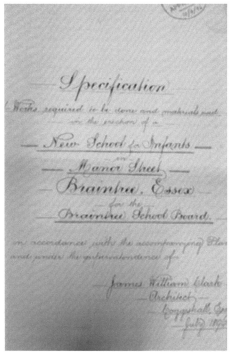

Photo 4.22 Cover sheet of architect's specification for new Infant building

In 1890 an inspector report suggests some improvements in furniture,

> 'There should be sufficient desk accommodation for the whole of the first class. This might be gained by taking desks from the present babies room and substituting a gallery which would be more appropriate for the little ones and give increased space. A cupboard with glass front should be provided for objects for the object lessons and these could be collected as far as possible by the teachers and children and with gifts from friends might become the nucleus of a school museum.'

Photo 4.23 Small room of infant building in 1981

REPORT 1892 – 'The room is rather crowded and one class sitting in front of another increases the difficulty of teaching.'

REPORT 1894: – 'The mistress teaches under difficulties but her skill and devotion to her work are worthy of all praise and she has produced some extremely good results. The school is however over crowded, insufficiently supplied with desks, the gallery is a very bad one being too narrow and without backs. The children's clothes are soiled by the boots of those sitting behind them. A letter frame and a large ball frame are wanted. I do not think the grant under Article 98 a of the code can be continued unless better accommodation can be provided.'

Photo 4.24 Spacious hall of new infant building

Desks became the norm instead of the benches, although more children could be squashed onto the benches in galleries. By 1913, Mr. Smith reports "It was neat rows of 2 seater desks of which there must have been 4 rows of 8 or 10 in the infants." The junior head reports 'New seats and tops to all the desks in large room. Great improvement on old benches.' Further desks in iron frames also came in 1898 then 'new desks arranged great improvement on the old desks.' and then again in 1911.

The old infant school

The old infant premises seem to have been a particular concern and led to the building of new premises which were opened in 1897. Mr. James William Clark of Coggeshall, Essex was the architect. Mr. Clark made drawings of the old building as well as designing the new one showing two wings had been added to the original. Photo 4.20

Photo 4.25 Funeral procession of Edward VII showing the three buildings in place

A builder's sketch made between 1874 and 1887 also indicates these extensions and has

Photo 4.26 Older pupils with backdrop of old infant building

further suggestions for demolishing walls to increase space. Photo 4.21

Noise must have been a problem as even with separate rooms they had no doors, a problem modern open plan schools have faced. They tried curtains indicated by the entry: 'Repaired the curtains between the big room and classroom this afternoon after school.'

Heating was problematic, firstly by a fire in some sort of stove. It was used in order to 'dry the walls but coals are so poor that it is not to impossible to keep the fire alight for any length of time.' The stove was inadequate. 'The smell of sulphur from the school room stove is again very strong this morning. The stove needs repairing.' Later the stove was replaced but, 'The school room has at times been much too warm since the hot water pipes have been fitted, there being no means of regulating the heat except by opening the doors and windows.'

'Defects in ventilation commented on by HMI have been attended to and school can now be ventilated without a draught.'

The log book records they 'commenced work in the new infant school.' Even in their new building the infants accommodation was problematic. The small rooms remained a problem until numbers dropped so much in the late 1980s to enable all the children of the school to be accommodated in the main building. A photo taken in 1981 shows the room still occupied by 28 children with their fire exit determined to be through the window. Photo 4.23

REPORT 1911 – 'Except for 3 short periods in each week the two lower classes are kept seated in their two small classrooms on the 3 occasions when they do use the main room. The children crowd the small space available being taken together as one class. Means should be devised for more frequent change of rooms for the classes especially for the more general space in the main room.' The main room was spacious. Photo 4.24

Photo 4.27 Junior classroom in large room showing fixed hall partitioning 1981

Photo 4.28 Junior classroom in large room showing folding partitioning and track of removed partition 1982

After the new infant building was erected and occupied. the juniors also made use of the old infant building. The head 'arranged classes as far as possible and commenced permanent work in the old Infant room with standards one and two work in the large room much more convenient and pleasant.' The 1904 Managers' minutes record the insurance costs for the three buildings.

'new infant school. £1,500
old infant school. £600
main building. £3,400.'

The co-existence of the old and new infant buildings can be seen in the photograph of King Edward VII's funeral procession in Braintree. The gables of the 1862 building can be seen behind the old infant building which is alongside the new building. Photo 4.25

The 1910 photograph of children, taken in the grounds also shows another building close to the main one. Photo 4.26

But the conditions in the old infant building were not improved.

Photo 4.29 Marching corridor, a long room made with glass partitioning 1981

REPORT 1899 – 'The ventilation of the old infants room is extremely defective and on a visit to the school the atmosphere was found to be in a very vitiated condition. This additional room is also ill adapted for teaching purposes so long as two classes have to be taught therein.'

In 1900, 'Temp in old infant room this afternoon 91°F .' They tried improving the ventilation 'of the old infants room by means of some Tobin's pipes and the classes rearranged to diminish the number accommodated. The lighting is also better for the additional window has been put in during the year.' Tobin's method brings the outside air into rooms through pipes which are carried some feet up the sides of walls. Presumably they can be introduced into an existing building as a cheap way of improving ventilation without putting in more windows.

Photo 4.30 Flooring changes in museum showing positioning of old partitions

REPORT 1908 – 'The west classroom is a very unsatisfactory building. It is not well lighted nor well ventilated at one end etc. etc.'

The partitions

A large hall and an ancillary small classroom were still the norm for schools in the Victorian period. The change from dealing with the children on the large space of the main hall to a cellular approach, that is individual classrooms, came in in the late nineteenth century and is still with us as we write. In order to change from one large teaching area to separate classrooms in 1906, three mobile partitions were erected in the large room and a glass panelled wall leaving a corridor alongside. The managers allocated the children to the various rooms which they also numbered.

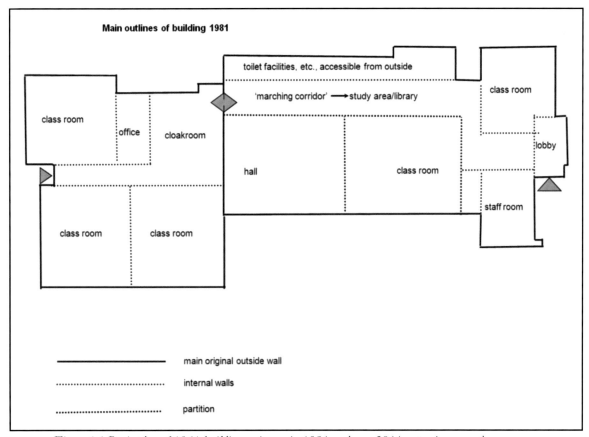

Figure 4.1 Basic plan of 1861 building as in use in 1981 and new 2011 extension, now the museum.

Room 1. Standard 4. 66 children-. at the west end
Room 2. Standard 1. 60 children
Room 3. Standard 2. 54 children
Room 4. Standard 3. 58 children
Room 5. Standard 5. 56 children – the room at the east end at the back
Room 6. Standards 6 & 7 66 children – the old infant school.

There cannot have been much room to move with these numbers. The older boys moved the new partitions to allow assemblies to take place. The infant school head asked the managers if they would consider partitioning the large room in the infant school at the same time but they would not. They offered the curtain instead. The caretaker was allowed to dispose of the old curtains from the main school and given 30s. – *£1.50* for his pains.

1906 HMI REPORT – 'It is understood that certain alterations are to be made in the premises and it is greatly to be regretted that the very unsatisfactory west classrooms are not to be included in the proposed scheme as it is of importance that these should be dealt with at once and give the children proper conditions of work. The head was occupied the greater part of the week in making arrangements suitable to the recent alterations of the large room into four divisions by sliding and fixed partitions. Eventually this will prove a great boon to the education of the children.'

'The new classroom arrangement is beginning to show improved results.' Photo 4.27, 4.28 & 4.29

These partitions stayed until the school closed although two were removed in the late 1970s. Evidence of their existence can still be traced on the floor of the main room of the museum. Photo 4.30

This unsatisfactory state of affairs of repeated reports of overcrowding prompted the managers to fund some new building. In 1909 it was reported that:

'The subcommittee are of the opinion that any alteration in the building should be in keeping with the south front elevation of the main room and recognize that any structural alteration to the existing west classroom would not be permanently satisfactory. They recommend that steps be taken to replace such a building with a new block, conforming to their first suggestion and that such block provide accommodation for 2 classrooms for 55 scholars each, a Headteacher's room, an assistant teachers common room and a girls' cloakroom.'

They recommended that Mr. Clark, the architect for the new infant school, be commissioned to prepare plans. They later went back to plans drawn up for three classrooms designed by the County Architect in 1904 - 5. 'They decided this would be cheaper, even after paying Mr. Clark for his work on plans.'

It meant 'Standards 3/4 transferred to Bocking School during alterations.' An extension was built at the west end and the old unsatisfactory infant building was eventually demolished. Later maps show the extension. It included cloakroom space, the small office and three spacious classrooms. Fig 4.1

One of the classrooms is still used for the re-enactments of a Victorian classroom, the office is still a museum office.

'The school has been much disturbed by the building operations but it is now settling down.'

When standards III and IV transferred to Bocking School during alterations the head records 'that the annual grant for 1911 and the fee grant was less because of fewer children being present.'

Lighting, heating and ventilation were still a problem in the main building which housed the bulk of the juniors. 'The ventilation of the classrooms especially when the wind is in the north or east is anything but perfect and frequently most unpleasant when large classes are in the room.'

REPORT 1894: – 'Ventilation in both classrooms is insufficient and the smaller room is not properly constructed or furnished and is greatly overcrowded. This cannot I think continue unless it is made more convenient for school work. The overcrowding also must be discontinued.'

REPORT 1896: – 'the room does not seem to be well lighted.'
Difficulties are mentioned with heating in the winter and the lavatories were a problem.

'Office accommodation for boys and girls is insufficient.'

'The children did not reassemble at the usual time on account of the closets being under repair.'

There were also 'many complaints from parents about the girls' playground.'

'This morning had to sweep water out through gate into the road before girls could enter. When the infants and some of the mixed school girls have the opportunity, this part of the playground is the rendezvous.'

When the extension was built, the managers put a fence down the middle of what had been the boys' playground across the road so that the girls could use half. The managers and the log book noted that, 'unfortunately the boys' and girls' playgrounds are very public and have poor surfaces.'

END NOTES

[1] Smith, 1987

[2] Gardner, 2002

[3] letter in ERO D/DO T32

[4] details of this can be found on the internet

[5] often called the Balfour Act

[6] Gardner, 2002

[7] Rowley, 1974

[8] Cunningham, 2002

[9] Smith, 1987

[10] Curtis, 1967

[11] Smith. 1987

Chapter 5 World War I and after 1913-1939

Background and context

This period is dominated nationally by the first World War, WW1 and the depression of the 1930s. Both impacted on Braintree despite its relatively rural situation, because of the heavy industry located in the town. It was a target for bombing – made possible by the invention of flying machines – both aeroplanes and zeppelins. Industry suffered and thus families suffered, during the depression. Despite this, the people of the town and the school, celebrated the coronations, promoted the empire and indulged in the new developments like widespread electrification, the coming of the cinema, increased motor transport and mobility. Lake and Elliot's, as makers of motor parts, thrived and Crittall's continued to successfully make their metal window frames for which they became well known. Courtauld's, however, wound down their Braintree activities. It is also a period when we are

Photo 5.1 A bird's eye view of Braintree circa 1920

89

lucky to have personal memories of what life was like at school and in the town as well as the 1987 letter from Mr. Smith.

> 'The cattle market still existed where the Town Hall now stands, with its cows, sheep and pigs and quite a lot of them had to walk up Manor Street and only the odd one went by horse and cart. The Penny Gaff showed the first films in Braintree and stood where the Post office now stands... before the Braintree Picture Palace was built.'[1]

An aerial photograph taken in 1920 [2] shows the original old school building with its 1911 extension, an area of trees or garden in from of the main room and a divided playground across the road. The cattle market area opposite the school is clear, as are St. Michael's School, the old building and a meadow area behind the school.

Motor transport coming to Braintree was not all helpful. A boy was knocked down by a car but luckily only suffered a broken arm and later the infant head had to give 'the children instructions respecting the danger of crossing the roads and the necessity of walking on paths. Drew attention to a little boy who was killed by a motor yesterday in Braintree .' A few years later it was reported that 'a Form I boy was knocked down by a Moore's bus during the dinner hour. He was killed instantly.' '...'s inquest – jury expressed view that all reasonable precautions had been taken to avoid such accidents.' 'HT attended funeral ...'s distressing accident has thrown a cloud over the whole school.' When the new bus park was built, the boys' playground lost a four foot strip from the east side to make room for the new access road.

The First World War

Mr. Evans, the head who took over from Mr. Davies on the 1st October 1913, stayed all through the war but had to claim exemption from service on several occasions. He 'received notice from

Photo 5.2 Mr. Baines' memorial

the secretary of the Education Committee that I am exempted from military service until July 31st.' and again 'Received notice that my application for exemption from Military Service adjourned from last Friday will come before local tribunal on Friday next at 6.10pm at Police Station.' He noted that his conditional exemption was continued and at the end of the war he left the school to take up another headship in Dorset. He lost staff, for instance, 'Mr Geo. Baines Cert. in charge of Std IV was replaced by Miss Cowell during his absence' and 'joins the army for the period of war.' Mr. Baines was sadly killed on July 4th 1916 and a memorial to him remains in the museum. Photo 5.2

'Mr. Rees, headmaster of Bocking Church Street Council School, having been accepted for military service, Miss Anderson, Cert. Asst., on this staff will take charge of that school during the period of war. We are already one short on the staff and appointments since the war are, in quality, not of high teaching power and efficiency.' When Mr. Rees was released from military service, 'Miss Anderson, temp. head of Bocking Church Street, returned.' Miss Anderson was acting head of Manor itself when Mr. Evans left, until the new head, Mr. Quick, took up the post in 1919.

An entry in 1917 points up the sort of staffing difficulties the war brought about. 'Took Std IV myself in addition to VI and VII. The difficulty of teaching two classes at opposite ends of the school must be experienced to be appreciated... Application has been made to the managers that a part of the summer holidays should be taken owing to difficulties of staff.' The managers refused, 'meanwhile the efficiency of the school is suffering.' Yet the following day, he appointed more staff to 'restore the staff to its normal numerical value.'

Mr. Evans also had family affected by the war. He 'was called to London on Saturday to see a brother who has been wounded and returned to England.'

He closed the school for a meeting 'in connection with the formation of a local cadet corps' in 1915. He then 'sent out 50 notices to old boys calling a meeting for Thursday evening next at 7pm.' '28 old boys gave in their names as desiring to become members.' The cadets drilled in the school, 'the first drill will be tonight Tuesday with another on Thursday and so on. 2 drills a week.'

It is often thought that air raids were a thing of the second world war, WW2 and even then, largely a problem for London or the big industrial towns in the north but Braintree had its factories and foundries making munitions and was clearly a target even in WW1. 'The Zeppelin raid of Friday evening with loss of life and the fact that other zeppelins passed over the town last Sunday night had adversely affected attendance.' 03.04.16 'The special constable turned people out of houses last night as a raid was expected & the parents & children spent a major portion of the night in byroads and as a result many have not come to school today. Those in attendance are nervous or sleepy & show inability to concentrate mentally.'

The infant log book records instructions from the managers to dismiss the children if the daylight air raid siren goes, using their own discretion as to the method of dismissal. 29.06.17

'Daylight air raid warning was given at 11.30am this morning. In accordance with instructions the school was cleared and children sent home.' 13.06.17

'Another air raid warning this pm at 3pm. Children sent home as per instructions. The all clear went at 3.50 when the majority of children returned.' 14.06.17

'Received notice from County Committee that when warning received that hostile aircraft have crossed the coast, the school children are to be sent home. Children dismissed upon five occasions this week owing to warning given attendance lowered on Wednesday afternoon owing to children being kept at home owing to "the raid".' 15.06.17

'Moonlight air raid scares have kept the children out of bed with resultant non-attendance at school next day.' 28.09.17

In 1916, afternoon school was brought forward while street lighting restrictions were in force during the winter. Gas consumption exceeded allowance under Household Fuel and Lighting order – 'informed caretaker of fact instructing him to exercise strictest of economy in use of gas.' Floor repairs were deferred for at least 3 years during the war.

Resources were affected including the years directly after the war. Economy in provision of extra staff to enable the head to be released from teaching was still grumbled about in 1921. Philip and Tacey school publishers, told the school 'that Farrington coloured chalks for the children's drawing could not be obtained during the war.' The pastels too ... Raffia work is

Photo 5.3 The Hicks family outside their shop in Church Street, soldiers from the Notts and Derby Regiment 1915.

discontinued in Class 1 owing to not being able to obtain material. Brown paper too is discontinued; this was used in all classes for drawing works with coloured chalk or crayons.' Shortages continued after the end of the war partly due to lack of materials but partly due to restrictions on non-perishable goods being transported by the railway.

The children participated in the war effort. 'Sold flags to children this week for Lord Kitchener day.' and collected 'plenty of Horse Chestnuts ... as requested by 'The Board of Education.' 'Stds V, VI & VII, about 100 in number spent the afternoon gathering blackberries as per request of Food Control office.' 'A blackberry excursion realised upwards of 70lb' and '120lb.' They even went 'collecting nutshells ... as they are required for the provision of charcoal for military purposes.'

In 1918 low attendance was noted as 'Children being kept from school to stand in food queues or mind houses while mother is shopping', although some boys were fascinated by the war.

Mr. Smith records:

"playing truant one day during 1914, we were told a lot of soldiers were to be marching through Braintree from Bishops Stortford and we decided we wanted to see. We waited in Coggeshall Road and the soldiers started to come about 9 o'clock am ... in full marching order and, as there was not much motorised transport about at that time of day and they only had horse drawn gun carriages and limbers... they were going toward Colchester ... about 3pm some red capped officer stopped the column and ordered the hedge to be pulled down where Ely's Garage now stands ... the troops went through the gap and made camp at the bottom where they built fires and had a meal and settled for the night only to move on again next day or the day after. The recreation ground became a transit camp for every sort of battalion you could mention, Scots in kilts, Geordies etc. We went back to school the next day and we weren't punished for playing truant although the headmaster and teachers were very strict, we never played truant again. From early in the war the casualties were very heavy and a lot of wounded soldiers ... were sent to St. Michael's. ... The VAD part was filled with soldiers ... and I used to have a chat with them. The children of Manor Street ... were asked if they could bring in anything to help them, like eggs and fruit etc.

The great War caused great misery and hardship and we had to go to school in worn out boots and shoes and clothes were patched so much they looked as if they were made of patches. My father was in the Royal Flying Corps and left my mother at home with 6 children and the married allowance was only about 30s. per week." [3]

After WW1

Following the end of the war, things seemed to improve but later came the depression of the 1930s. The announcement that Germany has agreed to armistice was received after the children had been dismissed 11.11.18 but was marked by a holiday and later remembrances.

'1 weeks holiday for Peace.' 15.09.19 'Peace holiday week given at this time for fruit gathering.' 19.09.19

'Day's holiday for "Armistice Day".' 06.11.19

'Holiday for first anniversary of Armistice day.' 11.11.19

'Special service was held from 10.45 to 11.30. All the children were assembled together and the two minutes silence observed. Suitable prayers and hymns sung. The headmaster then gave an address to the whole school.' 11.11.21

> A railway strike is mentioned on 29th September 1919 preventing a teacher returning from Suffolk and a teacher was late into school because the railway was disrupted by a coal strike in 1921. When holidays with pay first come in, children are taken away from school to go with their families and 'get away to the seaside' in 1927.

Milk was sold to the children daily at the end of the 20s and 1931 records 250 children paying for it daily but by June 1932, the depression began to bite. 'Milk club has greatly diminished in numbers owing to the great deal of men unemployed 80/day.' But 'the attendance this month has been remarkably good considering the large amount of unemployed in the town and the scant earnings of most parents. The health and condition of the pupils are remarkable. Careful inspection has been made to detect any signs of undernourishment due to the state of the labour market but we have failed to find any child in this condition. A very satisfactory state of things.'

In 1934 the government dropped the price of a third of a pint from 1d to ½d. The numbers taking it jumped from 50 to 245 when this happened. Later this is followed by 'The attendance is much below normal... some of the poorer families are pea picking. Owing to much unemployment in the district the problem of pea picking and the employment of children has again become important. This is the first year that so many children have been absent for pea picking.'

'Children are sent to the pea fields to eke out the family exchequer – first year since 1919 that so many children have stayed away for pea picking. Two pupils have been sent away to homes of recovery.'

In 1934 and 1935 'A collection of eggs for the Julian Courtauld Hospital, Braintree was made today. 738 eggs were sent.' The next year 630 eggs were sent.

Some of the pupils were very poor and played football in the street in their bare feet. One boy in Victoria Street where Ron Hutley lived, was so poor that he had to be absent from school because he had no shoes to wear. Some pupils' clothes were so patched up that they seemed to consist of patches. This is a similar comment to that of Mr. Smith about wartime children. The pupils managed to get work pea picking during the season and missed school; they also went gleaning and used the grains to feed their families' chickens. They could also go strawberry or runner bean picking.[4]

No-one had much money as quite a few of the parents were out of work. Clothes were handed down, there were no school trips and no-one went away for a holiday. The youngsters went scrumping in an orchard on Skitts Hill. They did have the opportunity to go to the seaside with the Sunday School. Robert Lockwood 1931-37 oral contribution.

Other occasions were marked with holidays, medals, lectures and songs:
'the wedding of Princess Mary, 1922.'
'wedding day of the Duke of York, The King's second son, 1922.'
'Wedding of HRH Prince George, the Duke of Kent and Princess Marina, 1934.'

'King's Silver Jubilee', 1935. 'All the children assembled on the lawn at 11 am where the headmaster addressed them on the meaning of the jubilee and the reason for celebration. Each child received a medal struck for the occasion bearing the Braintree coat of arms on one side and the portrait of K George and Q Mary on the other. These medals were given by Mr. G. Bartram the Chairman of BUDC'.

'Wedding of Duke of Gloucester and Lady Alice Scott, 1935.'
'Funeral of George V, 1936.'
'Coronation of George VI and Elizabeth, 1937.' Photo 5.4

Most young people now have no conception of Empire Day, a few of us living can remember it but it was obviously important in this period. Patriotism was expected – and taught.

'Today was celebrated as Empire Day. An address was given on the Flag and Empire on the lawn and patriotic songs were sung.' 21.05.20

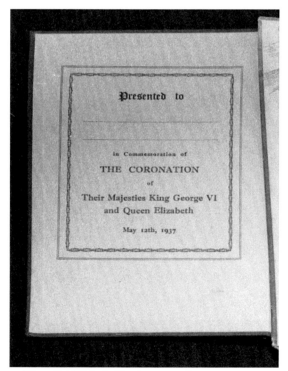

Photo 5.4 Flyleaf of book presented to commemorate coronation 1937

'At 11 o'clock, assembled on lawn, saluted the flag, had an address on Empire and on the flag from Rev, RJ Morgan and Mr Bartram as Chairman of BUDC.' 24.05.21

'Usual Empire Day celebration on the lawn Rev. Peel Yates was deputed by his co-managers to address the children, "Our flag and what it symbolises." 20 Empire medals awarded.' 24.05.27

The flagpole became dangerous and was taken down in September 1928 but quickly replaced.

Other events are sometimes recorded:

'Today an annular eclipse of the sun was visible at its greatest 9.45 am summertime. The whole school assembled in the playground at 9.40 and witnessed it. Lessons have been given on it during the week. Mercury was distinctly visible.' 08.04.21

'On Friday, a large number of upper school are paying a school visit to Wembley Empire Exhibition.' 02.07.24

'On the occasion of the Australian Cricket team visiting Chelmsford, 24 boys were absent all day.' 10.05.34

Governance and people

The managers continued to micromanage the council schools. They actually agreed that the headteacher could be present at interviews for assistant teachers – that is all his or her teaching staff in 1914. Any current headteacher would be appalled if they or relevant senior staff were not involved in any appointment procedure. The war is rarely mentioned in their minutes. Sometimes the military asked to use the school buildings for meetings or drill but it seemed managers saw school life continuing as normal.

Photo 5.5 Mr. Davies' memorial

Photo 5.6 Staff photograph 1926

Mr. Davies was not forgotten. 'A memorial to the memory of the late headmaster was unveiled by Mrs. Smoothy. The memorial which is fixed on the wall of the long corridor of the school was subscribed for by the old and present scholars of the school. A large number of old boys and girls together with managers staff and parents attended the unveiling. Mr. Sadd HMI and Mr. Row, Chairman of the Managers, spoke of the genial personality, tact and influence for good in Braintree of the late headmaster.' Photo 5.5

Mr. Evans had a difficult time during the war but was complimented.

<u>HMI report</u> 'The headteacher attends to his duties with much earnestness and is ably supported by his staff. The school is under effective control. The children are industrious and well behaved.' 10.07.14

Mr. Quick followed Mr. Evans until 1936. When he left, he thanked the staff for 'their kindness and conscientious work in a difficult school.' A county unattached head, Mr. Lucas, 'pending reorganization, a temporary master' took the school through the reorganisation from an 'all through' school to a junior school. Photo 5.6 includes Mr. Quick.

Alice Gray was the Mistress, head of the infants, from Sept 2nd 1889 and resigned through ill health in 1922. Miss Sharman, whom some still remember, took over. She remained head until Miss Jarvis took over in 1940. The memories of her headship can be found in the next chapter. Three more staff were mentioned with the reasons for leaving. 'Miss Rayner ... probably be leaving at Christmas ... to be a governess in a family .' '3rd class taught by Miss Wood have made some nice Christmas greetings.' 'Miss Andrews has given notice of resignation as she has accepted a post as wages clerk in a local factory at £91 per annum, about £1900 in present value her present salary being £65.' About £1300 currently, *26.03.18* you can see why she left!

 Mr. Smith remembers his first class, 'was Miss Chin's class and I believe one teacher used to look after 60 or more children.'[5] He also gives a list of teachers from his time at the school.

Teachers apparently started to get some professional development time – the junior head closed the school to allow them all 'to visit the Educational Exhibition at Colchester in 1924' and the infant head similarly to allow her staff to 'attend cinema demonstration of Physical training in 1935.' Female teachers such as Miss Fenton, having been teaching for over eight years had to send in her resignation 'pending her approaching marriage.' Teachers had to resign their posts when getting married until much later in the century.

There are a couple of old school magazines from this period in the museum collection. A poem from one, dated 1937, gives some interesting children's insight into the staff and the relationship the staff had with pupils in that they encouraged the writing of such things and their publication for others to read. Mr. Hoare was the acting headteacher and a Miss Nankivell a teacher at the time. A Miss Mankeville, though, is presumably the lady mentioned in the following poem not the teacher. Miss Mankeville is referred to in the log book in 1913 as being the 'inspector of nuisance in regard to the very unpleasant smell which renders the condition of Miss Hemming's room almost unbearable. The smell, that of decaying animal refuse, apparently comes from the garden 2 doors away, attached to Heastor's Butchers shop.'

Mr. Went, he has a car
    It goes by fits and jerks,
And every time he winds it up
    A bit falls from its works

Miss Nankivell, renowned of old,
    As a force is far from spent,
When all else fails rest assured
    She will trace them by the scent.

Congratulations Mr. Hoare
Monsieur le Président

HB you love so come above
    You are not broken but bent.

Keith Taylor leaves this term you know
    It makes us feel so sad
For who can tell what pains we'll bear
When the milk goes so quickly bad.

Two others whom we'll miss so much
    Amy Bateman and Kenneth Beck
No tea, no bell, we shall feel – well
    The ship has become a wreck.

Support staff, other than the caretaker, do not get a mention. It is not clear whether there were any, although cleaners were probably employed. Children brought a packed lunch or went home so dinner staff were not required. Mention of a receptionist or school secretary does not appear in the log books.

The school was still governed by a board of managers, who turned up on special occasions as well as meetings and also visited to see work in progress occasionally. Mrs. M.H. Tabor visited with her husband and reports low absenteeism, full classrooms and sees some good compositions on 'my favourite lesson.'

Parents

Parents visited to see work and sometimes made a nuisance of themselves.

In 1923 'a 'parents day' was held at school today. Parents visited from 10am to 12 noon during which time the timetable was followed. In afternoon 2pm to 3.45pm each class in turn gave a small performance of song, dance and recitation.'

'Having had occasion to punish – for misbehaviour and lazy work, the father visited the school this afternoon in a violent passion. He threatened personal violence and his language was so foul that I ordered him off the premises and sent for a policeman. For some time he refused to go and remained poring forth a volume of foul language but later removed himself.'

Children

The numbers of children are given in detail at the beginning of the war. 06.02.14

Place	Standard	Number in class October 1913	Revised Number February 1914
? small room at back	I	55	55
In main hall of building	II	36	38
"	III	36	38
"	IV	36	38
"	V	36	38
? new addition	VI	60	60
"	VII	60	60
"	VIII	48	49
Total on roll		**367**	**376**

Ages	Number
6-7	1
7-8	64
8-9	61
9-10	61
10-11	42
11-12	75
12-13	40
13-14	31
14-15	1

The school was reckoned to be full in 1922 with 368 on roll and attendance is calculated as 94.5%. When the new schools of Bocking Place and Chapel Hill opened, children left Manor but the number on roll did not seem to be affected. The school remained popular throughout.

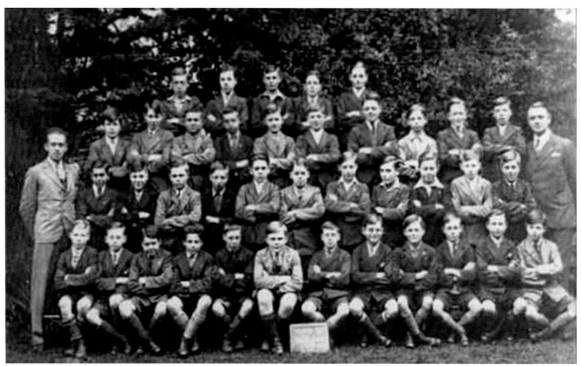

Photo 5.7 Older boys 1930

Photo 5.8 Older girls 1930

Children's successes and out of school activities are sometimes mentioned.

'---, 13 years saved a child --- 4½ from drowning in the R Blackwater. I am applying to the Royal Humane Society for recognition of this brave deed.' '4 of 5 entered gained scholarships.'

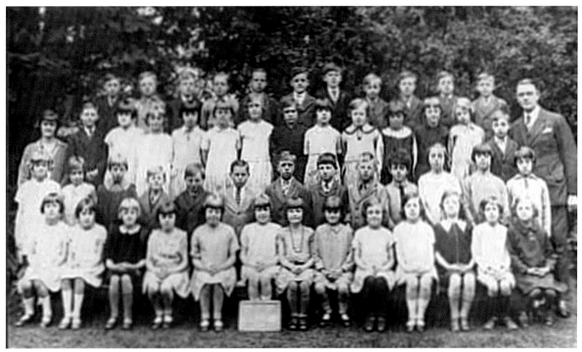

Photo 5.9 Younger juniors 1930

Photo 5.10 Infants 1928

'The school gained 5 out of 8 County Minor Scholarships offered for competition among the 62 schools in the Braintree and Dunmow area. This is a record for the school.'

Photo 5.11 Infants 1930

'3 Courtauld scholarships tenable at the County High School has been gained by pupils at this school.' These scholarships are the ones funded from the Courtauld endowment set up when the school was taken over by the board.

School uniform was introduced. 'School caps adopted, colours green and gold.' This doesn't seem to have lasted long although the 1930 photos of the older children certainly seems to show them more smartly dressed and more uniform than previously. Photos 5.7, 5.8, 5.9, 5.10 & 5.11

Teaching and learning

The major education reform of the period occurred right at the end with the introduction of distinctive secondary schools. The 1918 Fisher Act had already required that pupils of 11 and over should be accommodated in separate classes, if not schools and raised the school leaving age to 14. This distinction seems possibly to have taken place at Manor in 1922. 'The formal opening of the Intermediate School took place this afternoon when the Managers closed this school for the afternoon session to enable the teachers and children to be present at the ceremony.' The Hadow report, recommending a separation of primary and secondary aged children at 11 into distinct grammar and modern schools, was published in 1926. The first indication of reorganisation for Manor started in 1930 with a visit from an education officer and finally took place in 1938. 'This school ends today its long existence as an all through establishment. We lose today over 220 senior children and 5 members of staff – a crippling blow.' The education department in Whitehall seemed to have a low priority between the wars. Even instructions about air raid precautions for schools took two years from 1936 to 1938 to get published and no grant aid for building shelters was forthcoming until late 1940.[6] 1933 saw a further report recommending separate nursery and infant schools.[7]

The period saw a steady increase in professionalism and the development of educational philosophy, possibly because of the low profile of the government education department. The 1927 revised Handbook of Suggestions, published by the Board of Education, showed the advances made in curriculum thinking and design. Teachers' unions became more vocal and visible, especially the National Union of Teachers, NUT. Classrooms became more friendly places. The importance of gaining children's interest was recognised. Open days and weeks became more popular although we have seen that Manor had held these from its early days. Freudian psychology and the developmental theories of Piaget influenced teaching methods. The Macmillan sisters started their nursery school in this period; Susan Isaacs' books, still referred to by educationalists, were published. Magazines for teachers reflected the growth in ideas and were able to reproduce good pictures for display. Radio broadcasts started. The theme was education rather than instruction, especially for younger children, a shift of emphasis from the subject being paramount, to the needs of the child. It was the beginning of 'child centred education' which has become such a football in educational debate ever since.[8]

Mr. Smith describes his day in WW1 period as beginning at,

> "9am every morning ... with a roll call for the register, after which we had about ½ an hour learning religion and still remember the first hymn I ever learnt was "There's a friend for little children" ... We had no sex lessons. ... We also learnt to sing songs like "Sweet lass of Richmond Hill", "Ye banks and Braes",etc and when the war was on we learnt a lot of war songs like "Till we meet again", "There's a long, long trail a-winding", "Pack up your troubles in your old kit bag", etc. We had a little PT almost every day but no sport was played like football or cricket, just a few games like rounders. I believe the girls played netball and hockey and sometimes during the summer, we marched down to Rose Hill swimming bath. From 9am to 4 pm, it was all lessons and any games were played out of school hours." [9]

At one point in his letter he says,

> '...for a small school it can be very proud of its record and its teachers and I believe it is still a better way of teaching than the large Comprehensive Schools. We could write our names and work out Arithmetic without the lazy way they do now, which is by adding m/c or computers.'[10]

A day at school in 1937 is given in the school magazine of that year. It doesn't quite make sense in timing but the subjects mentioned are interesting:

Prayers   Arithmetic   Nature Study   Science   Handwork   12 o/c bell   PT
    3 o/c break   End of afternoon

Swimming, hockey and football are also mentioned.

Robert Lockwood was scared of the headteacher, who was the one who gave the cane. They had to learn things by heart such as tables and the notes in the music scale. The classrooms were bare, with about 50 pupils seated close together. There was not much bad behaviour because the teachers were strict - they would throw chalk at pupils when they talked.[11]

One teacher, Miss Nankivell, would hit pupils across the knuckles with a ruler. She tended to shout a lot which frightened the youngsters.[12]

The staff used record books and text books for 'the basics such as 'Jack's two term arithmetic, Herbartson's Junior geography and Modern Times History.' The school had schemes of work 'in English History, Geography, drawing and nature study. As promotions are made half yearly it is worth considering whether the syllabus should not be arranged to suit the circumstances. A certain lack of continuity which was noted in some of the work done in some subjects will it is hoped by now be rectified.' There was some flexibility – 'The timetable for the morning Empire Day 1916 has been adapted to admit of instruction in Imperial History and geography.'

In 1932 'An oak honours board was put in the long corridor. Two silver medals for "Character and general efficiency" endowed by GT Bartram.' Photo 5.12

MUSIC was more than just singing. In 1921 the entry reads 'A gramophone and records have been purchased for use in the art of listening and musical appreciation.' And in 1925 'Piano received today. We have held a rummage sale

Photos 5.12 The Bartram honours board

Photo 5.13 A Bartram prize from 1956 brought in for 1987 exhibition

and whist drive and the proceeds, together with the sale of an old piano and the contribution of £13.10s by the County Education Committee have enabled us to purchase the Riley Oak Piano £35.'

SENIOR PRACTICAL work seems to take place off the premises in some kind of centre. It is difficult to see, given the large number of children accommodated in the one building, where such activities requiring large apparatus and safety precautions could have taken place. The head noted 'Made up woodwork and cookery classes.'

'Visited woodwork class and saw work both written & practical. Made arrangements with instructor to keep in touch with work of boys. Owing to the fact that a difficulty has arisen in the Wed am class for cookery being accommodated this class will for the time being attend the Cookery centre on Wed pm.' 'Visited the woodwork centre re making of map rack. Took 4 of old hat racks to be used in making of map rack.' The school had a Singer sewing machine delivered so needlework must have been done in classrooms. 'The head wanted to keep bees at the end of the war but the managers thought it was 'inadvisable.'

PHYSICAL EDUCATION is increasing during this period although in 1929 the lack of playing fields was as ever, a problem. 'Recreation ground no longer available for school organised games.' However, the next year netball was started then the head 'attended a meeting at the education office to discuss the possibility of obtaining concessions for the playing of organised games on the Peace ground.' 'Football goal posts have at last been fixed in the Panfield Lane field. The hockey pitch to await further negotiation with the director.' And in 1935 Braintree Cricket Club grounds were to be used in the summer months.

The managers had had a letter in 1931 from the county authorities about the possibility of buying land behind the school. They hoped at the same time to dispose of the land across Manor Street which was used as a playground. They again decided against the purchase in 1938. Mount House owners then sold the land to the Roman Catholic Church, the grassland in front of the house being reserved under a regional planning scheme as private open space. They did enquire from Mr. Blyth whether he would make any land available – this is the land where Sainsbury's now stands – but nothing seemed to come of this. Maybe the demotion of the school from an all age school to a junior school and the threat of war prevented further land deal ideas.

There were interschool sports meetings sometimes 'on the High School sports ground kindly lent by the H.S. Governors.' Swimming was in an outside pool so stopped in the winter.

Outside activities and visitors continued to be part of the school curriculum.

'Took standards VI & VII to visit the poultry demonstration train at the station from 10-11am.' 16.11.16
'A school shop is started with dummy goods and bids fair to be an educational help.' 10.12.20
'Yesterday a lecturer from the RSPCA gave a talk to upper children on kindness to animals.' 08.05.25
'Lecturer from the League of Nations gave lecture to Std 6 & 7.' 15.01.29
'24 children attend quarterly session of ECC.' 19.05.37
'A party of 40 senior girls visited Messrs. Warner Bros to view coronation velvet and silk.' 23.03.37
'34 Boys on Educational visit to Ford Works at Dagenham.' 08.03.37
50 children were taken to the Isle of Wight for an educational trip in June 1938 and a grant from the county enabled all eligible children to go. 16.03.38
A library was started, 'Stds VI and VII have been provided with 48 books and standard V with 36 books.' 12.11.15 This was less than one each and by 1921, the next head tried again. 28.01.21
The children were taken to the cinema for 'a show of educational films.' 17.03.21 'the film "Livingstone" 19.02.26 "Northern Lights" 21.10.32 'Film depicting life in China and Japan' 08.10.26 and a ' "Tale of Two Cities" .' 19.11.36
The HMI report at the end of 1929 commented on a well-managed school with 'a little elementary science... but no facilities for practical work. Pleasing to note many social activities still form valuable part of children's training.'

A school inspection is also subject for a poem in the 1937 school magazine:

It is a thing most wonderful
Almost too wonderful to be
That inspector should stay for three whole days
and should not frighten a child like me
And yet I know that it is true
They came and saw and conquered too
They toiled and yes, perhaps they wept
But they also smiled as children do
And so we hope they'll come again
To help us with our daily rhyme
We shall not mind if they are kind
And pleasant as they were last time.

Maybe a few Ofsted inspectors might like a copy of this?

Health and welfare

Infectious diseases still caused concern and drastic measures like exclusion or fumigation, even sometimes school closures were the result. It was still a time without antibiotics.

'Chicken pox' 17.12.15 07.04.16

'Diphtheria' 25.11.13 , 02.11.15 and 19.11.15

'Measles' 04.06.15 and then 'the attendance has fallen to 64%.' 28.04.26 The same date also records 'A wild beast show is visiting the town' so perhaps some children were pretending illness!

Scarlet fever meant fumigation. 'This precaution was considered urgent by MOH.' 15.11.21

The first log book recorded case of polio is mentioned in 1938. 'School closed prematurely today owing to an outbreak of infantile paralysis in the district.'

'Excluded 2--- apparently suffering from scabies.' 11.02.14

'Excluded --- for dirty head, sent verbal direction for cleansing same.' 09.06.14

'Ringworm' 08.10.15

Vaccination against smallpox was not universal. 'Medical inspection Form 1. 54 children, only 10 have been vaccinated.' 31.10.21

Influenza after the first world war killed more people that the war itself. Braintree did not escape.

'School closed by order of the Medical Officer of Health for the epidemic of influenza until Nov 18th.' 30.10.18 and 'as influenza still dangerously prevalent in the town and district the MOH gave orders for the closure to continue.' 18.11.18 Mr. Quick also succumbed and was off school for over a month. 07. 03–11.04. 20

There were occasional accidents. In 1914 '--- had tip of little finger pinched off in a dual desk.' And in 1924 'One of the wall cupboards fell to the ground after school hours, one of the teachers
having a narrow escape.'

There was health education on various subjects, usually done by visitors. 'A lecture on temperance and the effect of alcohol on the body was given by Mr. Addison to children of Standards VI and VII this morning.' and 'Miss Dowdall attended and addressed the children on the care of the teeth.'

Dental care was taken seriously, 'The first dental clinic was held today when 18 children were treated – principally extractions.' 23.03.27

Building and environment

HMI reports continued to point out the defects of the building.

> 'The premises undoubtably make effective organisation difficult. There are classes of about 50 in each of the 4 classrooms, accommodating 36 children. Two other classrooms are thrown into one for a class of 59. Standards VI and VII numbering in all 62 are taken together in one room. It would seem desirable that in a school of this size Standard VII should have a separate teacher and a course of work different from that of Standard VI.' The head comments that numbers incorrect.

> 'It is greatly to the credit of the staff that in spite of the handicaps imposed by a difficult building, overcrowding and the necessity for interim promotions, the department is worthily upholding its reputation for industry and solid achievement.'

In 1919 the infant building was not without criticism. Mrs. Tabor, Chairman of Managers said that she felt sure that 'teaching would be more effective if this large room were divided by a partition.' There were 195 on roll at the time. The 'Ed. Committee decided not to proceed but to temporarily limit the numbers attending my school to 150. No. on books 198.' In 1920, 'Chairman of Managers drew attention to badly ventilated classrooms.' In 1921 the large open room meant no 'games in school as there is a difficulty of having one class at work while the other is having games and dancing in the same room.' Mrs. Tabor also commented

gallery was removed in 1922 and finally in 1923, the head reported that 'Work on partition progressing.' It resulted in a 'Note from office that numbers can go up to 200.'

The managers discussed amalgamating the two schools in 1938, with the idea to make the large room in the infants into a hall and the two smaller rooms to be used for staff but it was not acted on.

Mention of replacement burners for the gas lighting was mentioned in 1913.'The result is better light but one of the burners is too far forward and affects the light of the teacher. A paper shade somewhat remedies matters.'

Mr. Smith's letter tells us that there was no electricity in the school while he was there during WWI 'only gaslight and was supplied by Braintree Gas works.' He left in 1919.[13]

The managers discussed the possibility of electricity being installed in 1926 but there is no further mention of electricity being installed until 1929 when 'Electric light point for magic lantern is now ready for use.' Later 'Electric light has been extended to 8 points – 5 extra .'

The turret or steeple with its bell got a few mentions. The turret has to be repaired in 1931 and in 1933 the bell ceased to sound when the caretaker pulled the rope. The managers decide

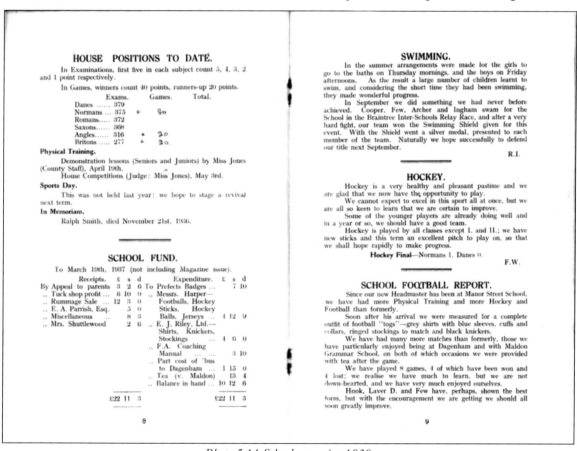

Photo 5.14 School magazine 1930s

Photo 5.15 Exterior of school late 1930s

not to restore the clapper, so the bell stopped sounding. It rang again for the beginning of term September 1936. The managers worried that there was no lightning conductor on it at one point.

The outside toilets were always a problem. They froze in winter and flooded when it rained. During the 1930s however, new washbasins for the girls were installed and new lavatory equipment.

The junior playground was unsatisfactory. It was not tarmacked and in the winter the 'Thaw created mud in playground 3" thick, children not sent out to play. Playground needs a good coating of gravel.' Later on the head commented 'In spite of efforts during the past year to improve the playgrounds, they are after heavy rain unfit for children. The children's shoes after play were plastered with yellow mud the surface being quite soft and sodden.' They tried to improve matters with a 'New rainwater drain put in the playground to carry off surface water, in 1928 part of the area, if not all, was grassed as the 1936 report reads 'new panther lawnmower received today.' The infant playground near the main new building, However, was tarred and 'retarred and sprinkled.'

The heating was unreliable whether coke or gas. The boiler could clinker up or burst and being in an underground room at the back could also flood. At the end of the war gas, coal and coke were in short supply causing children to be sent home as the school was too cold.

World War I and after 1913 – 1939

The proximity of the school to the market came up frequently in the managers' minutes. It was sometimes the parking of vehicles and sometimes the noise. By 1937 a police constable was on duty at lunch time and before and after school on market days.

In late 1938, the managers reported a query from the Chief Constable concerning the lighting of school in the case of war, they decreed schools would not open after dusk. Then came the news of the outbreak of another war.

END NOTES

[1] Smith, 1987

[2] Now in the Frith Collection

[3] Smith, 1987

[4] Ron Hutley 1926-34 oral contribution

[5] Smith 1987

[6] Gosden 1990

[7] Martin 2004

[8] Cunningham 2002

[9] Smith, 1987

[10] Smith, 1987

[11] Robert Lockwood 1931-37 oral contribution

[12] Ron Hutley 1926-34 oral contribution

[13] Smith, 1987

Chapter 6: World War II and after 1939-1980

Background and context

This period is dominated nationally by the Second World War, WW2 and the subsequent recovery period.

Technology expanded, in 1945 the telephone and the wireless arrive at the school. The wireless was used, among other things, to pipe the schools' religious service to individual classrooms.[1] Later an electric gramophone, television, then in 1976, colour television were all installed. New lighting was installed in 1958.

Braintree itself expanded. As the new housing estates were built to house a growing population following the end of the war, new schools were built locally to them. Even when the head of Manor left to take up a headship in John Bunyan School in 1965 and took 119 children and 5 staff with her, the school continued to be popular and full. Twenty-three more transferred when the new John Ray Infants School opened in 1968. The new schools could easily have spelt the end to an old school in an old town centre but somehow Manor retained its popularity. It seemed to stand in people's minds for tradition and stability. When Great Bradfords School opened, a few more transferred and the threat of closure of the school became public – but still the school remained popular.

Recovery from the war was slow as the country was bankrupt and rationing of some products still existed until 1952. As the country gradually recovered, employment was better and standards of living increased across the board. However heavy industry gradually declined as cheaper imports replaced local production. Restrictive practices in mining and engineering came under fire from the government and Braintree saw firms gradually close. Warner's Silk factory did make the coronation robes for the 1953 coronation of Queen Elizabeth but could not maintain production against overseas competition and by the end of this period, it too had closed. As car ownership increased, shopping centres opened and individual high-class shops such as Braintree had developed – for example Crittall and Winterton's and Joscelyne's – were also losing customers and eventually had closed by the end of this period.

The second world war at Manor

Schools from Edmonton were evacuated to the town at an early stage and classrooms were taken over en bloc by the visiting schools. The admission register kept for these children records their names, 93 of them and the schools from which they had come. Some of these schools have disappeared but others still thrive in what is now the borough of Enfield. The schools listed were as follows:

Raynham,   New Street   Montague   Northumberland Park

Bush Hill Park   Hazelbury   Croyland   Downhills

Houndsfield

Both log books record the late opening of the school in the September of 1939:

'owing to the outbreak of war and the reception of evacuated children school did not reopen until today instead of Sept 4.' 18.09.39

'A number of evacuated children from Edmonton have been accommodated in this school. They are using the small south classroom.' 19.09.39

'In consequence of the state of war 24 children were admitted from outside the town, 14 of whom were evacuees from districts other than Edmonton, whose school migrated here as a whole.' 18.09.39

'81 children from Edmonton occupied rooms 2&3.' 19.09.39

22 evacuees are mentioned again in August 1944 but there is no note as to when they left in between.

Photo 6.1 Exterior of school early in WW2

Braintree again suffered from air raids as the local industry was known to be involved in the production of munitions. Before the war even started, the headteacher, Mr. Hoare, suggested building air raid shelters in both the playground in front of the school and the one across the road and connecting them with a subway under the road. By October 1939,

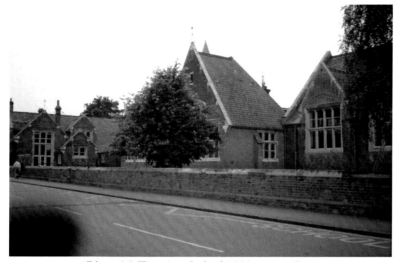

Photo 6.2 Exterior of school 1981 – no railings

the air raid warnings were sounding, 'Children gathered in the long corridor and took part in school and other songs. In the interval, the headmaster read a story.'

In spring 1940, the junior school reopened early 'as holidays were cancelled by the government when risks of raids became imminent on German invasion of Holland and Belgium.' The log book records that parents took children away from school during August for their own holidays and then towards the end of the month the school had to close – not for holidays but in 1941 'as par instructions of Chief Education Officer as air raid shelters not complete, neither has glasswork been given sufficient splinter protection. When school opened last September outside windows were covered with gummed strips. This is not now thought sufficient in consequence of developments. Estimates have been

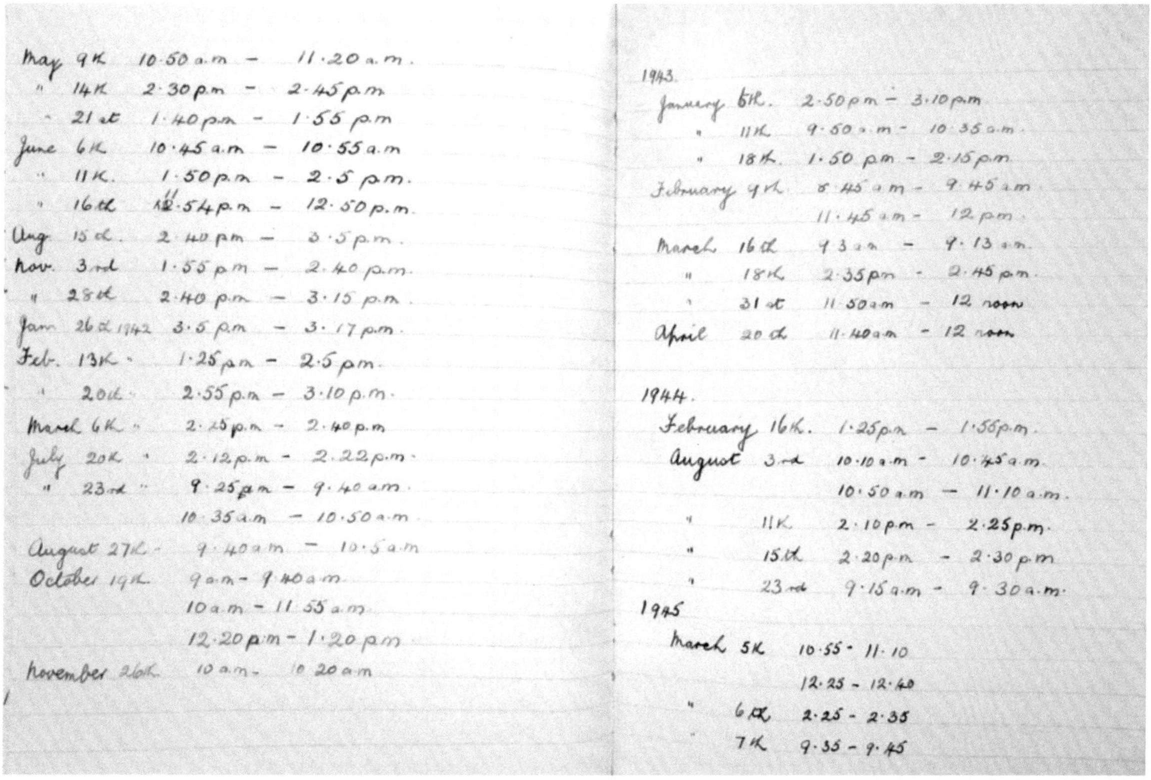

May 9th 10.50 a.m – 11.20 a.m.
" 14th 2.30 p.m – 2.45 p.m
" 21st 1.40 p.m – 1.55 p.m
June 6th 10.45 a.m – 10.55 a.m
" 11th 1.50 p.m – 2.5 p.m.
" 16th 12.54 p.m – 12.50 p.m.
Aug 15th 2.40 p.m – 3.5 p.m.
Nov. 3rd 1.55 p.m – 2.40 p.m.
" 28th 2.40 p.m – 3.15 p.m.
Jan 26th 1942 3.5 p.m – 3.17 p.m.
Feb. 13th 1.25 p.m – 2.5 p.m.
" 20th 2.55 p.m – 3.10 p.m.
March 6th 2.25 p.m – 2.40 p.m
July 20th 2.12 p.m – 2.22 p.m
" 23rd 9.25 a.m – 9.40 a.m
10.35 a.m – 10.50 a.m
August 27th 9.40 a.m – 10.5 a.m
October 19th 9 a.m – 9.40 a.m
10 a.m – 11.55 a.m
12.20 p.m – 1.20 p.m
November 26th 10 a.m – 10.20 a.m

1943.
January 6th 2.50 p.m – 3.10 p.m
" 11th 9.50 a.m – 10.35 a.m
" 18th 1.50 p.m – 2.15 p.m
February 9th 8.45 a.m – 9.45 a.m
11.45 a.m – 12 p.m
March 16th 9.3 a.m – 9.13 a.m
" 18th 2.35 p.m – 2.45 p.m
" 31st 11.50 a.m – 12 noon
April 20th 11.40 a.m – 12 noon

1944.
February 16th 1.25 p.m – 1.55 p.m
August 3rd 10.10 a.m – 10.45 a.m
10.50 a.m – 11.10 a.m
" 11th 2.10 p.m – 2.25 p.m
" 15th 2.20 p.m – 2.30 p.m
" 23rd 9.15 a.m – 9.30 a.m

1945
March 5th 10.55 – 11.10
12.25 – 12.40
" 6th 2.25 – 2.35
7th 9.35 – 9.45

Photo 6.3 Infant log book showing air raid warning record

given for curtain net on all glass.' Windows in the infant school were also covered with textile fabric after inadequate protection from glass splinters caused a school closure. Photo 6.1 shows the exterior of the school early in the wartime, with railings. The railings were removed from the north boundary in 1943. The 1981 exterior shows no railings. Whether they went along with those from the north boundary as a contribution to the war effort is not reported. Photo 6.2

September 24th saw air raid warnings and on the night of October 16th a real raid. 'An air raid during the week did much damage among houses in East Street, Albert Road and St. Mary's Road. Many children & Miss Wright absent as result of explosion of two land mines dropped by enemy planes last night. House demolished & people injured. Miss Wright spent the day recovering belongings from her partly demolished house.' 17.10.40 Warnings continued over the winter. The infant head recorded all the warnings of the war at the front of her log book. Photo 6.3

'The shelters were very cold – the day being wet and foggy.' 21.01.41 'During Jan & Feb 1-3 alerts almost daily – children accompanied am & pm and attendances recorded in notebooks. Mr. Moorhouse HMI called this afternoon to enquire if all the children were carrying gas masks.'

Then in 1941, 'owing to enemy action on Friday night the blast from H.E. bombs dropped on the town caused damage to the school as follows:

22 panes of glass broken, skylight broken

2 doors bolts and locks wrenched off

2 gates damaged

many slates disturbed or off roof

guttering over stoke hole and boys offices broken off

bricks dislodged from end of E. room inside chimney

coping stone cracked dangerous .

'The matter was reported at once & the workmen have been doing repairs during the weekend.'

'A representative from the Electric Light Co. called to view shelters and the installation of electric light.' Estimates for electric light in the shelters were gathered by the managers but memories of pupils from that time usually mention the lack of light and the teachers having torches so it is not clear whether electricity was actually installed. There is also some debate about where the shelters were located, in the main playground or across the road, maybe both? Tom Young[2] certainly remembers one in the front playground. He also remembers John Franklin bringing in comics to read and Mr. Young, the teacher, still reading them when the all clear sounded. 'Mr. Schofield, ARP Instructor called this morning 12 respirators were left in case of an emergency.' The managers reported that the air raid shelters leaked, which gives visions of not only dark but wet caverns, which, for small children, must have been very frightening.

The Post Office took over the infant premises 'for the Christmas rush in 1940.' This recurred in 1942 and again in 1943 although this time the log book reports 'staff allocated to other schools.' Presumably the children had an early holiday. The school also stored a quantity of bricks and material so that a field oven could be erected if there was an emergency. Other small things are sometimes mentioned like, 'The Brentwood Laundry delivered clean towels yesterday for the first time for over a year' in 1944. The shelters were finally demolished after the end of the war in 1947.

As in the depression, the school did its bit to help the community: '270 eggs collected for hospital.' 19.04.40 'Aid to Russia fund amounted to £2.7s.7½d.' 06.01.42 The junior school closed for a fortnight in the summer of 1940 'owing to exceptional conditions arising from out of war... for peapicking season.' Peapicking is mentioned again after the end of the war in 1945, this time for '5 weeks holiday.' Approval was given in 1942 for the fire prevention 'people to use the building for sleeping, washing and using the lavatories during the night.' Previously in 1941 'The District Clerk accompanied by the local food control officer called this morning to make arrangements for storing food supplies in case of emergency.' These were checked in 1944 by an official from the Ministry of Food, so the process had continued for some years.

It wasn't all gloom and doom for the children in 1940: 'To commemorate war weapons week in Braintree, Clown Bertram gave a short entertainment in each school today.' The cinema continued to provide entertainment and education for the children: 'naval films'; 05.03.42 performance in connection with the local 'Wings for Victory' week; 20.05.43 educational films to celebrate 'Salute the Soldier week.' 09.05.44 The children went with a couple of teachers in September 1944 'to an exhibition of materials and articles made for the war by Courtauld's works at Chapel Hill Mill.' 21.09.44 Even mentioned is 'the Rev. John Puttenell is giving a puppet show to the children as a special Christmas treat.' 21.12.44

After the war

VE day, 8th May 1945 the end of the war in Europe, meant the infant school closed for two days. Miss Jarvis reported, with an entry in red ink 'School reopened today after having three days holiday because of the unconditional surrender of the German armed Forces in Europe. Tuesday was celebrated as VE day Victory in Europe Day.' 11.05.45 Then finally she wrote for 'VJ day, it was announced at midnight that the Japanese had accepted the terms of the surrender. Two days of public holiday have been authorised.' 15.08.45

Photo 6.4 Mrs. Hilda Carver weaving purple silk velvet for the coronation of Elizabeth II at Warner Mill in 1952

There were further celebration holidays:

'marriage of HRH Princess Elizabeth to Lieutenant Philip Mountbatten.' 19.11.48

'King and Queen's silver wedding anniversary.' 23.04.48

'wedding of Princess Margaret to Mr. Anthony Armstrong-Jones.' 05.04.60

'Queen's Silver Wedding.' 20.11.72

'Royal wedding.' 14.11.73 of Princess Anne

'Queen's visit." 28.05.71

'The Festival of Britain' in 1951 and 'the Death of King George VI' in 1952 are also mentioned. The coronation of Queen Elizabeth II got special treatment. '128 children from the top classes and 6 members of staff visited Warner's factory this afternoon to see the velvet and fabrics made for the coronation.' 19.02.53 'School closed for Whitson and coronation holidays.' 22.05.53 'Coronation tea parties are to be held this afternoon in the infants' school and canteen hall. Beakers and souvenir books are to be presented to each child by "Miss Braintree".'04.06.53

Photo 6.4

'Preparations completed for the celebration of the school's centenary – actual date of opening

in 1862 was April 7th.' To celebrate this occasion, Miss Jarvis also wrote up a history of the

118

monotonous sounds and words, busy boys and girls will be found grouped round tables, reading from interesting, illustrated story books or browsing over books in the class libraries. The teacher will be moving among the children, giving individual help where-ever possible. Painting and Singing will not be done merely to "break the monotony" (quote from Log Book dated 23.1.65) but for the specific purpose of illustrating a story, making a mural, depicting a scene, and of course, for pure enjoyment.

Film strips and films are shown on the school projector to bring home the realities of geography, history, science etc. A regular feature in the school curriculum is the Wireless lesson.

Visits to outside places of interest are made whenever possible and conversely, people qualified to speak on their work or travel are invited into school to talk with first hand knowledge, to the children.

All aspects of education have their place, academically, culturally and physically. Regular lessons in physical education games and dancing play no small part in developing healthy children. Small children, suffering from malnutrition or rickets are a thing of the past.

Regular visits by the school doctor, nurse and dentist are part of the normal routine.

Most parents play a great part in the education of their children, showing interest in the work of the school and co-operating with the teachers to the benefit of their children. Children are sent to school looking trim and neat in their school uniform of royal blue and grey. Gone are the drab dresses, petticoats and starched pinafores worn by girls; the knickerbockers, stockings and stiff collars of the boys.

The children are proud to be pupils in a school rich with tradition. For from this school, which celebrates its hundredth birthday this year, have gone forth many scholars who have brought honour to it. Many have acquired positions of importance, but for the vast majority their tribute to their old school is proving they can live as good, honest citizens.

It is always a great joy to welcome back old scholars and know that the beginning of their education-for-life, commenced here, in Manor County School.

Schofield, Printers, The Avenue, Braintree. Phone 1234

Photo 6.5 Page from Centenary Booklet by Miss Jarvis

school using the old log books. A copy of this is in the museum. Photo 6.5

FURTHER DEVELOPMENTS

The 1970s are now known as a time of unrest. Manufacturing industry and mines were closing, strikes in protest at potential redundancies or low wages were increasing. This could affect the school life. For instance in 1971, 'a post office workers strike has caused some disruption of normal school business.' And again in 1979 'School forced to close today as result of action taken by members of NUPE.'

'The divisional office phoned re a phone call reporting that a bomb had been placed in a mid Essex school & suggesting that school should be evacuated. This was carried out.' 29.02.72

'Another bomb scare was reported. It turned out to be a hoax.' 02.03.72

The so-called winter of discontent of 1973 was noted by: 'News came today from Mr. Case that the school was to close until further notice as all gas supplies cut.' The staff, however, agreed that from March 12th the school would be open on a voluntary basis for two hours in the afternoon. It 'continued for two weeks two days. The response and support was magnificent.' 'The Braintree College offered a classroom at the annexe in East Street. This will be used by the reception infants every afternoon. Every morning from Tuesday 12th this will be used in rota by all the junior classes.' School reopened on 28th March 1973.

Governance, finances and people

The upper school changed radically in character on October 3rd 1938. The senior children had left in the summer and would go on to separate secondary accommodation, purpose built, in Panfield Lane, unless they had passed to go to the High School. Manor opened in the main building as a 'Junior Mixed Establishment.' Even the 'lawn mower and roller were transferred to the senior school.' The temporary head remained in post in the new junior school at the outbreak of war until Miss Jarvis was appointed head in September 1940. The loss of older children did not seem to affect the infant school in any way.

What did affect the infant school, was the next major reorganisation, the amalgamation of the infant and junior school under one head in 1952. Miss Sharman, the feared and by all accounts rather fearsome, infant headteacher, retired on 27th July 1951. The junior school log book records a presentation to her by a Mr. Rhodes of 'a gold watch from the parents of & pupils past and present". Miss Jarvis was made the 'temporary headmistress with 191 on roll.' The 'amalgamation of the two schools subject to approval' took place on February 28th 1952, with Miss Jarvis as headteacher. At this point the school formally became known as Manor County Primary School. The infants remained in the separate building, with their own toilets, heating and staff kettle – and their own culture too but the buck would stop with the new headteacher, housed in the junior school.

Miss Jarvis tried for other headships. She noted an interview 'for headship of John Bunyan School' in 1953. Eventually she got the headship of the newly opened John Ray School in 1965. She took with her 5 staff 'inc. deputy and Wyn Phillips &119 children.' Wyn Phillips had started as a member of staff in 1963 and later went on to be head of Great Bradfords Junior School for many years. 'Mrs. Want, new head, Mr West, deputy both' took up posts in September 1967. Great Bradfords school was late in opening and the transferring children and their new teacher actually had a class at Manor until their school was ready. In 1971 Mrs. Want noted:

> 'The staff quota for this school was left in abeyance until the exact number transferring was known, consequently we are commencing the term with larger classes in some cases, some of the rooms being unable to accommodate more than 35 children.'

Mrs. Want retired at the end of 1972 and Mr. Tyler was appointed head. A few years into his headship in 1976, he had the sad job of telling 'staff that Mr. West had collapsed and died the previous evening. ...10 years a deputy.' The following September, 'Mr. Tyler was seconded to Kings College to complete degree studies. Mr. Broad was appointed acting head.' Mr. Tyler was away a year, returning 'after completing a B.D. degree.' A cup was given in memory of Mr. West which became an award given weekly for one of the then four houses.

Photo 6.6 Friends of Manor Parents' Association Saturday morning fête

Staff

Miss Ludgater is recorded as retiring in 1951 after 42 year's service. Marion Cathcart is mentioned in the log book as gaining 'admission to Braintree County High School' in 1950. Marion, as Mrs. Booth, went on to become a teacher at the school in 1967 and was still doing supply cover until the closure, when she retired. She continued her association with the school as a Friend of the Museum. Her three children also came to the school. Jenny Rumbelow neé Clark is also mentioned. She taught at the school before her marriage and after an absence 'for one week owing to her marriage' returned to continue teaching at the school. After having breaks to bring up her family, she taught until her retirement, also when the school closed.

The post war period saw the beginning of the moves by teaching staff to establish themselves as a profession on a similar footing to doctors or lawyers. The unions started to take action. In 1968 the 'teaching staff have opted out of dinner duty. Work of MDAs mid-day assistants has been reorganised so that an extra one has been appointed it will be possible for them to supervise school meals by themselves.'

'NUT sanctions – dinner duty and out of school activities.'

Parents

Parental violence is nothing new or Victorian. In 1968 the head reports, 'After school today, Mr. B--- called and asked if I would give him the address of the attendance officer. I said "yes" if he came with me to the office. On arrival at the office door I saw Mr. L--- waiting to give me some books so I said to Mr. B--- "Here is the man you want to see." Mr. B--- went up to Mr. L--- & said "You stopped my daughter in the street & nobody is going to do that". He struck Mr. L in the face. Mr. L. attempted to defend himself & a fight ensued. I phoned for the police. Eventually the police arrived and Mr. B--- was taken to the police station for questioning.'

Parents also formed an association, Friends of Manor, which raised money for the school with fetes and events. Photo 6.6 shows a fete in the school playground on a Saturday morning, timed to catch the weekend shoppers.

Children

Children were rarely mentioned by name but in 1947 '---- swallowed a pencil.' There is no indication of how he/she did this or what the outcome was. In 1953 '--- swallowed a 3d piece. He was sent home to be taken to the hospital to be X–rayed.' In 1941 an incident of theft from a teacher's desk, after a break-in, was mentioned. It consisted of 2s.6d, some sweets and milk taken. Boys were later seen and questioned and some balls and tops in their possession were recognised. Jane Well's memory of her time at school in the 1960s included not being allowed to speak to the headteacher, unless she spoke to you first.

Teaching, learning and curriculum

The first major education reform of the period was the 1944 Education Act, which actually came into being during the war. The war had brought change in governmental attitudes to education, which spurred a few people into action.[3] The act meant that government began to take a much greater interest in education, having left it to local education committees and boards since the 1902 Education Act. 'Under the Education Act 1944, all junior schools become known as primary schools from 1.4.45.' By junior, the government meant those schools which had children from ages 5 to 11 at that time. There remained and still exist, separate infant and junior schools, with separate buildings and governance but the period of education from 5 to 11 remains the primary period of education, distinct from secondary and tertiary.

The post war period saw amazing changes in style, the partial reversal of which has taken place in the years since the closure of the school. The whole idea of children being receptors for teaching, sitting in rows and listening – hopefully learning from the wisdom of the teacher became tempered with the understanding of the ways in which children learn.

Instruction was still the backbone of teaching but children's ability to discover, explore, investigate and question was incorporated into the methods used. The 40s and 50s had been a period of gradual recovery from the austerity on WW2 and the 60s brought a period called by some 'swinging' others 'euphoric.' This release into a period described by prime minister Macmillan as being one where people "had never had it so good" overflowed into education. But this freedom of approach led to yet more problems for Manor. The building had no outdoor areas to investigate other than tarmac or passing transport; the furniture was ill suited to group work. The new schools being built were more spacious and more flexible, much more suited to creative, scientific and exploratory work, with water in every classroom, outside grounds, reception areas and proper staff and head's rooms. Major reports from committees looking at primary education in general and special educational needs led to changes in practice. Parental expectations were raised as they themselves became more educated and standards of living improved.

Miss Jarvis described the school in her 1962 pamphlet:

> *'Visitors to the classrooms no longer hear the squeak of slate pencils but see children writing their own stories and accounts, with colourful illustrations, in books proudly preserved to show parents on "Open Day". Instead of rows of children chanting monotonous sounds and words, busy boys and girls will be found grouped round tables, reading from interesting, illustrated story books in the class libraries. The teacher will be moving among the children, giving individual help wherever possible. Painting and singing will not be done merely "to break the monotony" quote from log book 23.1.1865 but for a specific purpose of illustrating a story, making a mural, depicting a scene and of course pure enjoyment.'*

She goes on to mention visits and visitors, physical education, games and dancing. One ex-pupil, David Kemp remembered a guinea pig running round the classroom under the heating pipes.

The period saw a steady increase in professionalism and the development of educational philosophy. A research based report into primary education[4] gives us a comprehensive picture of education at the time. Subsequently, the report was vilified because of many misunderstandings and misinterpretations of its contents. Some schools took the developing ideas of child based education to mean relaxing the role of the teacher. Some very public disasters, particularly in the William Tyndale School in London, created a lot of concern about teacher freedom over the formal curriculum. This led over the ensuing years to considerable research into actually how teachers teach. The end of this period in the school's history was also the end of a period of teacher freedom. Throughout this period, it was believed that "the teacher knew best".

Photo 6.7 Some of the readers in use in this period

The Bullock report on the teaching of English [5] which was well received by the teaching profession, was reported to the Managers by Mr. Tyler in November 1978. He told them that Manor teachers maintained a balance between the didactic and the exploratory, possibly tending towards the didactic, basic skills and teaching were seen as important. He referred to it as the "middle way". He added that there was no streaming in the school at that time but children got individual attention. There were however two year groups in many classes. He referred to language development, not English. He told of guidelines for the infant classes in mathematics and English. Mathematics in the juniors was structured and common policy was discussed. Reading books of the time can be seen in Photo 6.7.

Mr. Tyler saw the intake as a 'few high fliers, a good average and some remedial children.' He also reported that volunteers were working in the infants.

Manor seemed to keep a structure along with the developing creativity. It retained certain traditional values of discipline while embracing all sorts of interesting activities. However, the teaching and learning was still very formal. Christine Wiggins recalled that they had to learn everything by heart especially their times tables and how to do punctuation. She recalled that one of the classrooms was heated by a large coke burning stove which had a guard all round it. The children would dry their socks on this after they'd walked to school in the rain. There were, she recalled, a number of poor children who had holes in their socks, shoes with holes in and poor clothes. Gillian Panton remembered that a poor child might be given clothes by the school. Caitlin Phillips remembered that there was one little girl who was bullied because she was so smelly; she had dirty clothes and matted hair. There was by this stage, a uniform: a royal blue jumper and a grey blazer, though this was not compulsory. There was a small clothes shop where one could purchase these. Punishments still tended to be hard, you could get hit with a ruler across the hand and pupils were put in the corner if they were naughty.

Science lessons were introduced for a year in 1958. Brian Panton recalled that he was enabled to do science when he was eleven because he was in the "B" stream and the subject was not considered suitable for "bright" pupils! The science clearly did him a lot of good because he went on to become an engineer. The children also went on nature walks still, along the disused railway line but on one occasion two boys got stones and smashed a resident's greenhouse windows so the nature walks ceased! Caitlin recalled chanting her Maths tables; Maths was taught by rote and an abacus was used. The pupils still wrote with ink pens with italic nibs and there were ink wells on the desks. Pupils learned poetry by heart and there were weekly mental arithmetic and spelling tests. Quite a few pupils took the 11 plus each year and by the early 1970s, science did feature on the curriculum, though not in a big way and was, taught by Eric Broad. The way English was taught varied between the different teachers.

For instance, one class learned famous speeches from Shakespeare by heart and other pupils found the reading books incredibly boring. Although there was no library, every pupil had a history and a geography book which they kept in their desks which had lift up lids.

While the cattle market continued to be right by the school, the youngsters nipped there after school – Mike Baker recalled that he was terrified by the great big farmers with their sticks. They would also sometimes go to the cattle auction or to the Phoenix Café where they could have lovely big ice creams. When Mike was small he remembered being terrified when his Mum left him there; he was also intimidated by the high windows placed so that the children couldn't see out. Mike felt that the teachers in the 1960s were quite Victorian and some were very strict insisting that they all sat up straight in rows. The headteacher in the 1950s, Miss Jarvis, was thought to be immensely old by the pupils, Margaret St. John Coleman recalled. She bought her dachshund to school and he stayed in her office all day. The pupils were enabled to take craft subjects; they did embroidery or made papier maché puppets and the top juniors in the 1950s prepared a school magazine. On Friday afternoons, the infants had a "quiet time" when they could do puzzles or jigsaws or make pictures with coloured shapes. In the lessons involving "nature talks" they were encouraged to bring things, - interesting leaves or flowers for instance, which they had found. Angela Gridley, neé Cooper 1949-1955 remembered writing on slates with chalk but didn't know whether it was because of a paper shortage or a style of teaching. Small whiteboards with water-based felt pens as well as tablets, even laptops are commonly used in classrooms today.

There were many games that the children played at break – hopscotch, skipping or "it", hoops, spinning tops; "British Bulldog" was a game involving everyone running from one end of the playground to the other trying to catch a person in the middle; "Donkey" was a game in which one played with a ball seeing how many times the ball hit a wall, while the pupils also played "kiss chase" where the only safe place to indulge in this was the outside toilets; there was also a game called "knicker chaser" when the boys tried to get the girls' knickers down!

Unfortunately for Caitlin Phillips, she was badly bullied because she came from a middle class background, was quiet and had her head in a book: none of the bullying she was subjected to would be tolerated now; she was terrified by girls who would chant rhymes at her in the playground or who would take her pens and pencils from her desk or rub out her work or scribble on it. She was also pinched and nipped by other girls. She has a negative memory of the Infants school where she was terrified of the teacher because she shouted at the pupils. One little boy wet himself and he was humiliated in front of the class. Other pupils were bullied; for instance, one girl who was well developed for her age was bullied the whole time. Caitlin managed to retreat into herself by having an imaginary black friend; presumably she associated the discrimination which black people endured with the bullying she received. If a pupil was really naughty, there was corporal punishment, a slipper for the girls, cane for the boys. She recalled one pupil who had to rinse out his mouth with soapy water. In the school assemblies the head would talk for hours and Caitlin Phillips remembered that for a whole term he took the theme of the Lord's Prayer; he would take a line for each assembly and discuss this. Many of the children found this very boring. Others like Terry Lawrence 1950-1954 said he had fond memories of a lovely school that certainly put him on the path of a

Photo 6.8 Gymnastics in the canteen

Photo 6.9 Sports day at the Tabor Field

good education and success in later life.

Mr. Broad was the acting headteacher for a year while Mr. Tyler gained a divinity degree. He was, according to the pupils, very strict. However, when he wasn't looking, the pupils would chew bits of paper, make them into a ball and then ping them up to the ceiling with a ruler where they remained. The ceiling was evidently covered with these bits! The pupils had secret places where they could practice kissing such as behind the piano or in the outside toilets. Many of the pupils did not like the school dinners which they were forced to eat; in particular they hated glutinous puddings such as semolina or tapioca.

MUSIC
In 1945 'Country dancing and Morris dancing were performed by Manor St. children at the official opening of 'Braintree Week' in commemoration of the 750th Anniversary of Braintree receiving the charter.' They were able to learn the recorder after school. Singing and dancing were practised in the school hall. 'Mr. Butler played the mouth organ to them which was fun.'

In 1955 'An Eisteddfodd was held this afternoon' and in 1957 a 'Braintree Schools' music festival at John Bunyan. Mr. Rees-Davies conductor, Mr. John Georgiadis violinist.' was recorded.

PHYSICAL EDUCATION
The school was still using the recreation ground for organised games in December 1939 but did not start using it again until 1948. The school paid 8s. 40p a week to use the recreation ground but they had to walk to it. Equipment was also used for PE as in 1941 '4 new balancing benches and 1 set jumping stands received today.' The PE lessons were very basic, the school being very handicapped by lack of space or grass. Mike Baker recalled there was little equipment though Brian Panton recalled bean bags and benches and Caitlin recalled walking round with a bean bag on her head: they used "smelly" black rubber mats to work on. Brian remembered that they got changed for PE in the hall. Jane Wells remembers doing maypole dancing in Blyth's meadow in the 1960s. In 1953, the managers looked into hiring a field at the end of Coronation Avenue for playing fields but then had a report that the

Ministry of Food required the field as grazing land for animals prior to slaughter – it was adjacent to the local abattoir. Photos taken in the 1980s show gymnastics taking place in the canteen and a sports day on the Tabor Field. Despite the limitations the school maintained its standards and in 1961 'won the Primary Sports and Relay Shield.' One Facebook ex-pupil remembers the canteen floor being very cold. Photo 6.8 & 6.9

A note in the 1976 Managers' records made in 1986 indicates that changing facilities were made available at the Braintree College Annex, adjacent to the Tabor High School playing fields in Courtauld Road. Clearly arrangements had been also made to use the grounds for older children's sports. It entailed walking with the children along Manor Street, up Railway Street to the cross roads and then down Courtauld Road. At that time, Railway Street was the main ring road for Braintree, although a one way street and all traffic, including large commercial vehicles, had to pass that way. Thankfully, no accidents were reported during this activity.

Photo 6.10 Mural of The Lyon in Braintree Town Hall

GENERAL INTEREST

'A third group of children from class IIA were taken this morning to the post office and instructed by the postmaster on the internal workings of the P. Office.' 29.04.49

'Mr. Barry, an explorer from the Antarctic Falkland Islands dependencies gave a talk to the top class juniors this afternoon.' 08.07.49

'Visit to Railway Stn.' 06.03.50

'Visit to Police Stn.' 13.2.50

'Classes IA and II visited Chapel Hill to see the Hogarth Puppet show this afternoon.' 05.06.50 'Classes IVa, IV &III' went the next day but a child caught her little finger in a car door when being transported.

Photo 6.11 Exterior of canteen 1981

Photo 6.12 Interior of canteen set for lunch

Photo 6.13 Kitchen of canteen in use 1985

'A day in London – a trip on the river in the morning visits to Westminster Hall and Westminster Abbey, St James' Park, Buckingham Palace. The children saw the Queen drive out to review the Police in Hyde Park. Tea was arranged at the Strand Corner House. After a walk back along the embankment we embarked in coaches and arrived back in Braintree at 7.15pm.' 15.07.54

'Trip to London – Tower of London & State procession with Queen, D of E and King Feisal of Iraq.' 17.07.56

Braintree has connections with the first American immigrants. The Mayflower sailed in 1620 but in 1632 The Lyon sailed from London with people from Braintree on board. In 1957 'Mr. Wicksteed, second in command of Mayflower II which sailed to commemorate the first voyage talked to the top classes and showed coloured films of Mayflower II at Plymouth Massachusets. America.' Photo 6.10

In 1979 'Edward Blishen visited and talked to children about writing.'

Residential school journeys for the top juniors were started. Children went for the week to Norfolk, Salisbury and Dover, travelling by coach and staying in specialised youth hostels.

Health and welfare

The provision of school meals had expanded since the Liberal government had enabled the provision of free meals to those in need after 1906. Lunches were taken by Manor pupils at the C. of E. canteen situated in Fairfield Road. This was not easy. In 1942 'Mrs. Tabor called this afternoon to discuss with me the difficulties presented in conducting children to dinner.' Then 'Miss Sudbury commenced duties today as an escort for dinner children, plus performing the washing up of milk beakers.' It took time to get to the church school – the location of the dinner hall, so arrangements were made so that the children went to the second sitting, thus 'avoiding interruptions to morning sessions.'

Following the 1944 Education Act, school meal provision was made compulsory. As a result, more schools were provided with canteens, largely in prefabricated Horsa buildings. 'Mr. Broomhall from Co. Architects office spent the day here investigating plans and drainage re building of school canteen kitchen.'

The managers reported that the C. of E. canteen in Fairfield Road could not cope with the number of children who were staying to dinner in 1947 so a Horsa building was eventually provided in the children's playground across the road and Manor Street School Canteen was opened in 1948. 'Dinner was served in two sittings 12 noon–12-30.' This increase was part of the expansion of the welfare state during the Labour government following the war. 'Canteen staff appointed Cook, ass. Cook, kit. hand, ass. kit. hand, 1 class C and 2 Class A counterhands.' Current research indicates that the children's diet of that time was more nutritious that that eaten by many children today. Photos 6.11, 6.12 & 6.13

In 1946 another vehicular accident was reported. A 'boy's foot run over by a lorry at the junction of Baker's Lane and Chelmsford Road.' This was such that the 'boy's foot was amputated.' Given the open nature of the school grounds, perhaps the following accident of 1941 was not unexpected. '...received a bite from a dog which went in the girls playground.' Accidents happened in school, for example, a child bit his tongue when he 'omitted to lower his desk seat prior to sitting down', he slipped and caught his chin. A doctor saw him but he did not need stitches. Another child cut his forehead on the iron stand of the desk, which reportedly healed well.

The reports of illness almost completely died away. Vaccination was widespread following the introduction of the National Health Service. 47 children were vaccinated against diphtheria early in the war. There was however an outbreak of polio in the 1950s and 4 children caught it. It was during this period that vaccination against polio was introduced.

Children were still sent away with scarlet fever. Maldon Isolation Hospital is mentioned, German measles, whooping cough and chicken pox outbreaks are still mentioned and impetigo was a cause for exclusion. A mastoid operation is mentioned. The school had a nurse, "Nutty Nora"! The pharmaceutical developments made during the war had hastened the availability of antibiotics. But drugs for treating tuberculosis were not available until the

Photo 6.14 Infant classroom 1982 showing partition and lighting suspended from false ceiling

early 1950s. Sadly, a 'Little girl of 5 died from tubercular meningitis' but in 1947 Miss Jarvis, in her centenary pamphlet, said

'Small children suffering from malnutrition or rickets are a thing of the past. Regular visits by the school doctor, nurse and dentist are part of the normal routine.'

Building and environment

The school canteen also provided a place for indoor PE and whole school gatherings. No mention is made of regular assemblies but in 1946 the whole school go to 'the Co-op Hall for school play – song of Hiawatha.' In 1948 'the room that had been used as a hall has now to be used as a classroom. This will affect singing, dancing and PI physical Instruction lessons

Photo 6.15 Assembly hall in large room showing remains of partitioning at ceiling height, folding partition removed 1981

until the Canteen Hall is opened.' David Kemp mentions the pushing back of the partition between the classroom in the large room for assemblies.

At Christmas time 1948, 'a nativity play was held' in the canteen hall and the 'whole school had a Christmas party' there. In September 1950, the canteen is used by each class in turn as their classroom is decorated.

'Mr. Bishop called re loud speakers for every room.' Three were fitted along with a new wireless in November 1952 and two in the infants in February 1953. These were still in place in 1981!

There were continual minor improvements but nothing to really deal with the fundamental problems of the building and site. The infant log book records the dimensions of the classrooms in the infant building in 1949. The two small rooms were only 280 square feet and the two main rooms 630 and 850 square feet with the partition in place. The local education authority and parents would expect 30 children in each of those spaces.

In 1980 'Suspended ceilings fitted in Infants' to conserve heat in the high old building. Sadly, this not only took away the lofty architectural features of the old building, its spaciousness

Photo 6.16 Urinal for boys, using back wall, , 1981

which can be seen in the old photos but also a considerable amount of light. While making the rooms warmer, it took away the light from the high windows and the managers had to request the sloping of the ceiling around the windows to retain a little of daylight. Nevertheless, lights were often on all day, every day even in the summer. The false ceilings were removed when the building was remodelled for the museum and café which now occupy the building. Photo 6.14

The partitions built between the classrooms in the large old hall were large folding structures, reaching from floor to ceiling of the main hall, which folded back

Photo 6.17 Girls' lavatory with fixed wooden seat pieces 1981

when the hall large space was required. In 1979 Mr. Chaplin, the caretaker, was about to move them one evening when 'the central screen in the main hall collapsed. He escaped, luckily, with bruising to the shoulder. The result could have been a tragedy.' A 'decision was made to remove subsidiary screens from the hall and rehang the middle one', thus retaining two spaces rather than four. The westerly two spaces were retained as a hall and the other end as a classroom. Photo 6.15 shows the remains of the partition at ceiling height. At the same time, the similar screens in the infant building separating their large room into two teaching spaces were 'to be permanent.'

Photo 6.18 Wash hand basins for use by girls and female staff 1981

Toilets

One of the points of vulnerability of the school was the back wall. Blyth's meadow became an open car park in 1965, School Walk made one way and later in the 1980s, Sainsbury's came and tidied the car park. Previously, it had just been open space with a small lane running behind the school. The lane itself was an ideal place for loitering and gaining easy access to the school. Occasionally cars overran the car park and went straight into the school rear wall. The toilets were fitted in behind the school with the boys' urinal actually on the back wall. It was a very tight site, so the toilets were a vulnerable area. Photo 6.16

Photo 6.19 Portaloos in playground across the road

This wall at the back was actually demolished on one occasion– for a reason not stated in the log book but presumably through some accident or vandalism and the boys' urinal was demolished with it. This then meant in 1969 'the rail in front of the school was removed in order that the junior boys could use the infants' urinal.' On another occasion in 1962, a car 'left in Blyth's meadow car park without the handbrake on, rolled down the slope and crashed into the school fence.' 1977 saw the 'Rebuilding of wall next to infant toilets because dangerous', and in 1979 'At some point this past week a section of the fence at the rear of the school was hit and broken. It is to be assumed that this may have happened on Thursday during the course of the day and as a result of the dreadful road conditions.'

Photo 6.20 Only internal source of hot and cold water in junior building

The toilets were not only vulnerable to major accidents like these but were still very vulnerable to frost. They froze in February 1969 and the school had to have 'an exceptional closure due to no toilet facilities being available.' The weather was bad again in March 1970,

'Heating non existent and it was impossible to wheel coke. The toilets were frozen. Permission was asked to close the school. Notes were sent home with the children informing them if conditions didn't improve there would be no school the next day. 'Weather conditions slight better today, staff all prepared to open school but so few came that it wasn't worth opening. Six of those children who arrived stayed & had a school dinner since their parents were not at home they couldn't be sent back.'

Jane Wells, a pupil there in the 1960s, remembers the toilets as 'quite dreadful.'

The toilets were not only inaccessible from the inside of the building but were themselves rather unsavoury. Lack of handwashing facilities was mentioned in 1949 but there was reckoned to be insufficient room for improvements. This was especially a concern in the boys' area and that there was no access to drinking water for any children. In 1969, managers were asking for the area to be reconditioned and in 1972 were recommending plastic lavatory seats instead of wooden ones. Photo 6.17

Some of the Facebook comments are about the awful lavatories. The reconditioning and plastic lavatory seats did not actually take place until the 1980s.

New infant toilets were recommended by the managers in April 1979, these were eventually installed in the infant cloakrooms in 1981, meaning small children and their staff no longer had to go out in all weathers to the rear of the building. Another problem with toilets was during playtimes. Children playing across the road – traditionally boys but this was later changed to the older children – had no toilet facilities except to re-cross the road to the main school building. Portaloos were put into that playground in 1976. As they got older, they also were not the most savoury facilities but at least they were not the chemical variety, they flushed! Photo 6.19

'An Ascot water heater was erected over the sink in the East classroom during the Easter holiday.' This was still the only source of hot water for staff use until the closure of the school. Angela Gridley remembers monitors being allowed to wash up the teachers' cups and saucers when she was in the back room classroom. Photo 6.20

Various minor alterations were made from time to time.

'New gas heaters in west end classrooms.' 12.09.58

'School redecorated internally and externally.' 10.09.58

'New floors laid in Inf. & older part of J. building.' 12.09.60

'New washbasins in infants.' 10.01.61

'New boiler installed in the junior building.' 07.01.71

'A new gas fire in the office.' 10.09.71

'Resurfacing of the playground.' 06.09.72

'Contract to rewire the school.' 07.01.75

'Kiln installed in special kiln room.' 02.09.75

'Complete re-felting of a v. large area of roof.' 31.08.78

'Re-roofing of Infant building.' 06.09.78

'Painting completed and new shelves placed.' 23.02.79

'New roller screens in canteen.' 25.09.79

Inspectors reported on the inadequate facilities at the school. The inspection report for 1953 mentioned that the buildings used by infants were very inadequate and conditions very difficult. There was a small playground and a need for careful shepherding when crossing the road for music – but – it was essentially 'a good school where effort and goodwill are overcoming many difficulties.' In 1959 they reported that there were 355 children on a restricted site. 'The work of the school has for many years suffered from the ill effects of the peculiarities and deficiencies of the premises ... well equipped on the whole.' Also, that the standard of presentation made the classrooms 'attractive and pleasant places.' They commended the 'excellent handwriting.' They further commented that there was a 'strong feeling of unity in this school' accompanied by a 'cheerful survival, if not acceptance of the inadequacies and difficulties of the physical conditions.' The headteacher, teaching staff and caretaker were congratulated on the extremely satisfactory nature of the report by the managers.

Vandalism

A break-in was reported in the infant school in 1942, mentioned in the children section above, leaving 'two classrooms in great disorder.' The caretaker had left the key in the fire watchers' box the night before and this had allowed the miscreants to gain entrance. The junior head reported the games shed key missing as well. 'The police were informed and boys questioned' On August 11th the junior head reported that she 'had to attend the Juvenile Police Court .... re the case of ...and ...breaking into the school.' 'Vandals set fire to rubbish by office.'

Siting

The road between the boys', later older children's, playground across the other side of Manor Street became an increasing problem as vehicular traffic increased post war. But early on a 'Road Patrol commenced duties.' This was continued at all playtimes, arrival and home times until the school closure. It was later a combination of lollipop ladies and the police. The market often had stalls outside the infant building and beyond on a Wednesday and the taxi rank was on the other side of the road. In 1962, managers commented on the amount of rubbish left after the market and again in November 1979 Angela Gridley 1949-1955 remembered men cycling home from the factories for their lunch break and dads stopping to talk to their children over the front wall. Chris Pavelin early 1950s remembered the dads giving their children sweets at this time.

The movement of taxis caused a problem for the patrols and, I expect, the patrols were a nuisance to the taxis. Mr. Tyler notes that in 1979, he had 'a useful meeting at Town Hall re possible resiting of taxi rank' but it never was resited. The managers received a letter from Braintree District Council in May 1980 saying they had decided, in principle, to move the taxi rank. However, at the same meeting, the intention of Tesco's to build across the square was mentioned also the possibility of a Sainsbury's behind the school. Removal of the taxi rank would require a 'no waiting area' outside the school, which already had problems with parents parking before and after school.

Accommodation and numbers were a perennial problem despite the older children no longer coming to the school. The school was popular in its location – pupils could be dropped off on the way to work and picked up after shopping. It also maintained its reputation as a good school, so many applied from out of catchment area to come, despite the new schools being opened in other parts of the town. The junior log book notes discussions on the matter with the Divisional Ed. Officer on June 5th 1950. Miss Jarvis wrote in her centenary booklet,

'Today, in spite of many difficulties of cramped conditions, inadequate sanitary amenities and no staff or medical room, the building is kept in good repair. Electric lighting has been installed, a hot water system introduced into the infant building; new floors laid; improvements made to the heating system and all the woodwork painted in bright colours. Difficulties are surmounted. Pupils and teachers work happily together.' [6]

In 1971, the first public mention of possible closure took place. 'Mr. Primmer, County LEA Officer, addressed a meeting of UDC and headteachers regarding the future of primary education in Braintree 'A meeting was held in the school hall to explain the position as now visualised regarding the closure of Manor. As it seemed unlikely that the school will close for several years yet suggestions for improvements were made.'

The managers' minutes of June 1980 mention that the Education Development Plan envisaged closure of the school in a recent review but that the school should continue as it would be required for the foreseeable future. There was an agreement to continue supporting the school by providing new infant toilets and lowering the main room ceilings for heat conservation. There was even the possibility of a full remodelling project for the school. Towards this end, a conference of some kind was held in the summer of 1980.

In 1981 Mr. Tyler reported 'that Mr. Wilkinson County Inspector responsible for the school came to see me regarding the future of the school.' He had by that time been appointed to be headteacher at Kelvedon St. Mary's School and Mr. Broad had indicated his intention to retire in the summer. 'Mr. Gregory, Area Education Officer and Mrs. Warm, an Essex County Councillor, visited with reference to the appointment of a new headteacher.' Anne, Author,was interviewed for the post in the July and, when she accepted the offer of the post, a fortnight before the end of the summer term, was then told of the staffing problems the school was facing – no deputy and the placement of a teacher needing a fresh start. She was released early from her then post at Maldon County Primary School. She was never told either by the staff, parents, county or area officials of the possible intention to close the school until several years into her headship.

END NOTES

[1] Memory from DK

[2] Tom Young 1940-1946

[3] Gosden 1990

[4] Plowden 1967

[5] Bullock 1967

[6] Jarvis, 1962

Chapter 7 The last decade 1980-1990

Background and context

The final decade at Manor Street which saw the closure of the school in 1990, witnessed an era of enormous change both internationally with the end of the Cold War and with the establishment of the Conservative government which won three elections led by the 'Iron Lady', Mrs. Thatcher. Events such as the Brixton riots took place, which later in the decade were to lead to a realisation that schools needed to be aware of the need to counter racism in their policies and practices. The success in the Falklands war meant that the Conservatives were re-elected with an increased majority, while the miners' strike and the Brighton Hotel bombing by the IRA were partly instrumental in the government's decision to follow strongly centralised policies. These were to have an impact on Manor School.

The second Thatcher election success of 1979 introduced profound social and economic re-structuring. Winning two more times during the 1980s, Mrs. Thatcher felt that she had enough support to push ahead with a range of reforming policies. These neo-liberal strategies affected not only industry and commerce but public policy, which now underwent an emphasis on cost reduction, privatisation and de-regulation. The twin aims of education policies during the 1980s were to convert the nation's schools system from a public service into a market and to transfer power from local authorities to central government. Action was taken on three fronts: the curriculum which central government was not supposed to enter; the teachers, whose training and development was to be controlled and whose role in curriculum development was to be re-structured; and finally the local education authorities, whose power was to be weakened. By the 1980 Education Act more power was to be given to parents and governors rather than LEAs, new schools were to be created and existing ones closed.

Braintree was due to expand after the reduction of industrial employment and oil crisis of the 1970s. With the expansion of air traffic largely due to the popularity of package holidays abroad and the development of budget airlines, Stansted Airport was due to increase rapidly. Designated as London's third airport, it finally got the go ahead for expansion in 1984. Along with this permission came the promise of employment and a need for more housing in the local towns of Bishop's Stortford, Dunmow and Braintree. This along with the desperate need for a Braintree by-pass, released land for development to the east of the town. As with post war housing developments, the new eastern development would entail a new school

Photo 7.1 A class in the 1911 extension in 1982

being built. This was to be Beckers Green School. The long-standing problem of Manor Street School was put into this mix of local need for schooling, increased power for parents and school governors as they were to be known and a national proposal of increased market forces. The teaching unions were opposed to many of the reforms, proposing as they did to take power over what went on in the classroom away from them, just as they were becoming an all graduate workforce. By 1981, Eric Broad, who retired as Deputy Head then, said that many Manor Street teachers had the feeling that the school would be closing. Manor staff, unsettled by uncertainties in their profession as well as locally, were strong union members. Manor parents, many of whom were professional people, were vocal in their views. This mix made for interesting times for the last decade of the school. But the education of the children went on and they achieved a great deal both then and in later years as their testimonies have shown. Access to the log books of this time are embargoed at the time of writing, so our evidence is from verbatim and written accounts of the time and some tape, video and photographic sources.

People

Anne became head in 1981, taking over from John Tyler. At the same time Eric Broad had retired so Jean Michaels, a senior teacher, was acting deputy head until Malcolm Leeke was appointed deputy. There were four classes in the infant building and five in the junior building, with one class in the far end of the large room and one in the back classroom, three in the newer, 1911 extension.

There were about 250 children on roll. Anne left in 1987 to take up a headship at Tollesbury and, because of the proposed closure of the school, a new head was not appointed.

The school was led for two years by a what was then called a County Unattached head, Julia Smith. Towards the end of this time, Beckers Green School was built and the headship of that school advertised. Andy Jones was appointed to Beckers Green with a brief to close Manor and take the remaining staff, children and any resources that were still appropriate and usable, to the new school. The Manor County Primary School as it was then known formally closed in 1990, still with about 80 children on roll. Staff remained loyal and upbeat despite the closure proceedings, the lowering of morale through a fall in numbers, children and families leaving and the government imposed changes to governance and curriculum of the 1980s. Jane Wells described her time as a lunchtime assistant as enjoyable and being honoured to be on the staff. Bridie Williamson, a teacher during the later 1980s, also describes her time there with many positive memories.

She also mentions that the 1980s saw an enormous amount of parent cooperation, including in the classroom. The catchment area was only the area delineated by Coggeshall Road, Railway Street, South Street and the High Street. Therefore, few children came from the catchment area, the rest were from all over the town. James Elliston, who was in the last cohort to go all through the school, leaving in 1990, remembers his time as a happy one, despite the emotional upheaval for staff and parents over the closure proceedings.

Teaching, learning and curriculum

The 1986 Education Act gave governors much greater responsibilities and the 1988 Education Reform Act ERA as it was called introduced the National Curriculum and 'directed time' for teachers. The National Curriculum provided for a basic curriculum to be taught in all maintained schools – three core subjects – English, Mathematics and Science - together with six foundation subjects, history, geography, technology, music, art and PE. Teachers had virtually no say in the design of the National Curriculum or in its construction. Subject specialist groups on which teachers were represented were given the brief to independently produce a brief of what they thought should be learnt at each age. At primary level it was huge and unmanageable. By dividing the curriculum into discreet subjects, it made the integrated topic and project work difficult, if not impossible. Bridie Williamson described her teaching there from 1986 to 1988 as having 'a child centred approach, children were taught the three Rs very strongly, followed by an integrated curriculum around a topic based approach. It was really pre national curriculum, not the paperwork that there is today, we

Photo 7.2 A class of 28 children in one of the small infant classrooms in 1982

could focus time on teaching and individual needs of pupils. We used the library for books and the market for mathematics. We also did a wide range of art using many media and had music in the classroom every day.' By the end of the decade the national curriculum was to have an impact on Manor Street in the two years before closure.

For many years it had seemed to teachers at Manor that the facilities were old fashioned and that there were serious difficulties in providing adequate PE or in safeguarding the safety of the pupils and whilst most of the classrooms were adequate, it was difficult to create an exciting atmosphere with Victorian white tiles on the walls and windows that one could not see out of. Two of the infant classrooms held 28 pupils each which, with a teacher's desk, left no space for movement at all. Everything was stored on shelves around the room and the fire exit was through the window.

Anne, unaware of the threats to the future, continued to introduce new ideas. She had a very good knowledge of the primary curriculum and introduced many changes in the teaching and learning which took place at the school. The teaching had been, in many ways, very old fashioned and formal as indeed were some of the text books used. Steve Butler, a teacher at the school during the 1980s recalled that there were some English text books which were over forty years old in 1981. In introducing a more modern approach to teaching, several

Photo 7.3 Anne's last staff photo

Photos 7.4 Playground mathematics

of the well-established members of staff were opposed to the new regime which only added to the stress levels amongst the staff. Anne had to work hard to win them over. The staff got a real shock, Steve Butler recalled, when staff who were used to an informal curriculum were asked to produce lesson plans which

Photos 7.5 Playground mathematics

included three different levels for the differing abilities of the pupils.

1981 had also seen the publication of another major report into education, this time in
   mathematics.[1]
 Anne sent Steve Butler on a course at Brentwood Teachers' Training College to study how
to teach the 'New Maths' and she invited parents in to the school to come and have a look
at the new mathematical materials then available. The meetings were very well attended
although lots of the parents were nervous of the new teaching style involved. The New
Maths made a tremendous impact; pupil self-esteem improved and their understanding of
the subject made great progress.

Meanwhile, Science had barely been taught at all, apart from Nature Studies, so Anne introduced
science as a mainstream subject and staff were given help in teaching this. Such was the success of
this that the children entering the North East London and Essex NELEX technology competition
won three times. The older children one year designed a trolley which could be attached to a
wheelchair for supermarket shopping, encouraged by the local Tesco's which had opened
across the way from the school. Photos 7.6, 7.7 & 7.8

Trolley trio win place in the finals

LIFE could be easier for the elderly when they shop in Tesco supermarket — thanks to the ingenuity of three Braintree schoolboys.

The boys, all pupils at Manor County Primary School, have invented a gadget to connect a Tesco supermarket trolley to a wheelchair.

The invention has won them a place in the finals of the Nelex — North East London and Essex Science and Technology regional competition which are being held at Chelmer Valley High School in July.

The young inventors, pictured here, are Neil Reeder, 10, Oliver Phillips, 11 and Timothy Franklin, 10.

Report:
EVE SWEETING
Picture:
TONY TUNBRIDGE

Photo 7.6 Braintree and Witham Times report of entry into the NELEX competition

Photo 7.7 NELEX entry display and successful competitors 1984

Photo 7.8 The infants win a NELEX award 1986

Photo 7.9 A display of 4th year school journey work.

Photo 7.10 A display in the hall for open day

Photo 7.11 Carpeting in the long marching corridor

The problem had been that there was not really a set curriculum before the 1980s since the Standards of the late nineteenth century. Teachers taught what had been traditionally included in the lessons and they had to relearn how to formally plan a lesson only dealt with on their original training. The new deputy head, Malcolm Leeke, was able to show by example how it could be done. The classrooms were well equipped however, each classroom had separate bookcases for the children to use and the pupils had plenty of access to good reading. Although the walls of the classroom were tiled, nevertheless the teachers put up lots of displays, had open days and made the teaching space seem bright and friendly with desks grouped together for project work. Photos 7.9 & 7.10

A library, group work and study area was established in the long – so called marching –

Photo 7.12 Library provision in the long corridor

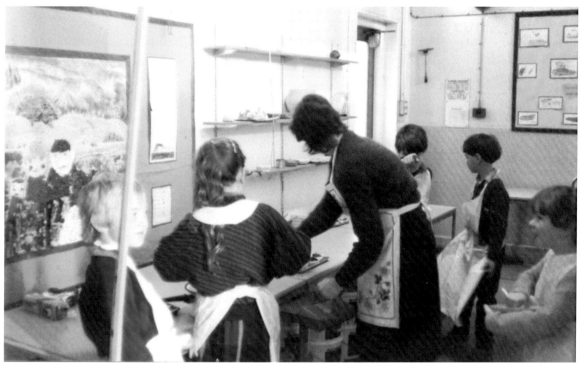

Photo 7.13 Group working area in the long corridor with a volunteer helper

corridor. It was carpeted making an enormous difference to the noise levels. Regular staff meetings enabled an agreed school approach to the curriculum to be established. Photo 7.11, 7.12 & 7.13

Photo 7.14 Children showing off working with a computer on an open day

Computers were introduced to schools during this time and each school was equipped with a BBC Acorn computer. This was housed in Manor in the long corridor study area and the older children were guided to use it. It was largely used for word processing and the introduction of the BASIC programming, which was thought to be its use at the beginning.

Electronic survey 900 years after Norman version

Children help compile new Domesday book

CHILDREN from Manor County Primary School at Braintree railway station, where they did some of their project.

NINE hundred years after William the Conqueror ordered a complete survey of the country, schoolchildren everywhere are busy helping to compile a new one. Only this time the Domesday Book will be an electronic one.

All over the country children are taking a close look at their surroundings – recording every house, field, pub, church – in fact everything that covers the ground. They are carrying out interviews and producing about 20 pages of text about their area.

Ten thousand schools are involved, mainly primary schools with support from some secondary schools.

The BBC's Domesday project is the largest interactive videodisk venture in the world and the first national survey ever launched by a non-Government organisation. It allows schools throughout the country to use microcomputers as research tools.

WORKING on the Domesday book entry, with the help of a computer, at Templars Junior School are, left to right, Adam Dawkins, Kim Frost, Daniel Moore, Karen Rowe, Kerry Earl, Aaron Coombs and Keely Patston.

Photos 7.15 Newspaper cuttings from the Braintree and Witham Times of the Domesday project involvement

The rapid development of computing meant that by the time the school closed, computers were appearing in every classroom. In 1986, the BBC ran a Domesday project. Each school participating was allocated a 2 kilometre area to research. Jean Michaels, an upper junior teacher, researched Stisted with her class. They entered the details into the computer, downloading the material onto a disk which they returned to the BBC. The BBC have now resurrected this material, which had been saved in an early obscure format. If you have a computer, type 'BBC Domesday project' into Google, insert the postcode of the school/museum 'CM7 3HW' and click on the rectangle just to the right of the spot marked Braintree. Here you will find all the contributions the Manor School children made. Their efforts were also recorded in the local press. Photos 7.15 & 7.16 Newspaper cuttings, Photos 7.17 & 7.18

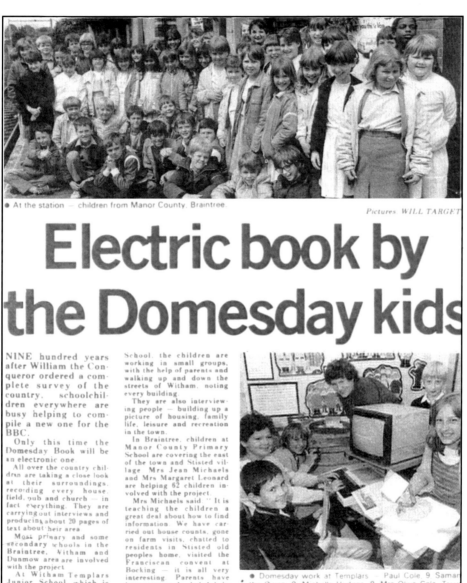

Photos 7.16 Newspaper cuttings from the Essex Braintree Chronicle of the Domesday project involvement

Photo 7.17 Children at the railway station doing their research

Photo 7.18 Children walking around Stisted fields for the project

Photo 7.19 Live musicians visit

Photo 7.20 A performance of Joseph and his Technicolcoured Dreamcoat

PE might have been difficult but Steve led the school teams to success in gymnastics. Photo 6.8

Music, established as a speciality in the time of Mr. Tyler, continued with groups, live musicians visiting and amazing productions of musicals like Oliver and Joseph and his Amazing Technicolour Dreamcoat. The infants also put on their own fully dressed productions. Photos 7.20 & 7.21

Photo 7.21 An infant performance of Hansel and Gretel

Things did not stop despite falling rolls in the second half of the decade. The 4th year, Year 6 children continued to go on week long journeys usually to Norfolk; they dressed up in seventeenth century costume for the visit of David Bellamy when he came to celebrate the 300th anniversary of John Ray's *Historia Plantarium* and then put on the pageant for the 125th anniversary. Interesting things like visits and visitors went on right up to the end of the school. Log book records found by staff of ERO give a few clues. There is a photo [8.1] of the John Ray visit in Chapter 8. Photos 7.22 & 7.23

'1st and 2nd years visited St. Pauls Cathedral and the whispering gallery and attended a creative dance performance at Sadlers Wells.' 19.11.87

'An owl and a python visited infant class prior to trip to Colchester Zoo.' 22.04.88

Photo 7.22 Setting off on a 4th year journey to Norfolk in 1982

Anne also finally ended corporal punishment and it was legally banned in 1986. It had still been common for teachers to give children a smack for instance. As far as discipline was concerned Anne stopped the practice of excluding naughty children from class and introduced a system of giving positive marks for good behaviour and achievement. The school was still very popular with parents and in the community; the strong parents' association - the Friends of Manor Street – continued, which organised the school fairs and

activities to raise funds for furniture or sports equipment. Photos 6.6 & 7.24

The building and equipment

The pupils still had to cross the road to go to the canteen for PE and lunch. Photos 6.8 & 6.11 The playground was divided, being either side of the road. A crossing patrol was present every break time and the taxis were still a nuisance. On one occasion, a taxi ran over the foot of the lollipop lady, who was very shaken but luckily did not suffer any broken bones. Newspaper cuttings 7.30 & 7.31

The market stalls still trickled down Manor Street to be right outside the infant school, making teaching difficult for them and test conditions for the juniors nearly impossible on one or two occasions. Bridie Williamson commented that local people enjoyed seeing the children play in the playground by the street but as a teacher she had to be vigilant to ensure

Photo 7.23 A boat trip in Norfolk on a school journey

Photo 7.24 The Friends of Manor, The Parents Association float in Braintree Carnival celebrating the 125th

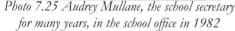

Photo 7.25 Audrey Mullane, the school secretary
for many years, in the school office in 1982

Photo 7.26 The school staffroom in 1981

for craft activities. The head and secretary shared the small office still used by the museum curator staff. Photo 7.25

The staff room was the one now used by volunteers, shop staff and others. Infant staff had been used to not coming into the junior building for breaks but Anne encouraged them to join in more, in order to facilitate a whole school approach. The desks were old and it was difficult to provide flat areas for group work. Gradually, funding dribbled through and they were replaced with flat topped tables and chests of trays for children's work and belongings. Other furniture was scrounged from the old Warner's factory which was being used as a furniture store by the LEA at that time.

As numbers dropped with the threat of closure, the small infant rooms were vacated and became offices for the head and secretary. The toilets remained outside for the juniors but were put inside in 1981 for the infants. There were still outside toilets for both staff and juniors and no washbasins for the teachers, apart from those used by the children.

The junior toilets flooded when it rained, Anne was told to bring her wellingtons when she first started at the school if it was raining in order to get to the toilet. In 1981 there were still

Photo 7.27 New access to junior toilets
from the long corridor

Photo 7.28 New roofing and
doorway for girls' toilet access

Photo 7.29 Boys' new stainless steel urinal
relocated more privately

157

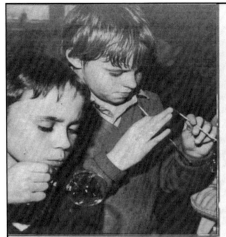

THE corridor library with shelves put up by parents.

...NDING out about bubbles in a science lesson — Marcel ...cCracken, 10, and Richard Naybe, also 10.

Not just a school — more a family

...was more than 100 years ago, ...862, that Braintree's Manor ...unty Primary School first ...ned its doors. And, says ...dmistress Mrs Anne Watkin... there is no reason why it ...uld not carry on for a further ...years or so.

Rumours, emanating from Braintree councillors, that the school is to close have caused anxiety among parents and staff, says Mrs Watkinson. The building may be old and inadequate but the school, with its cheerful family reputation is carrying on.

At this month's governors meeting Essex County Council firmly set fears at rest by stating: "There is no intention of closing the school." If a replacement building is to be found then such a project would have to compete with other replacement projects with limited money available. The Avenue site is not large enough, a site at Tabor High School cannot be considered at the moment and as yet no other suitable site has been identified.

"The important thing," said Mrs Watkinson, who came to be headmistress at the school just over a year ago, "is that people realise the school is not closing. We are here to stay."

However, there are accommodation problems — and Mrs Watkinson hopes Essex County Council will consider improvements a priority.

To start with the five to 11-year-old children have to cross Manor Street every day to have their lunch in a temporary wartime canteen where they also have to do PE.

In the junior part of the school the children have to use antiquated outdoor toilets. Only one of the nine classrooms has a sink in it and two classrooms are too small for the optimum number of children.

There are no playing fields and the children face a ten-minute walk for a game of football or any other sports.

The heating system is hopelessly out of date and cannot be controlled, and Mrs Watkinson has no office. "The school really needs tens of thousands of pounds to bring it up to date," said Mrs Watkinson. "The lack of sinks in classrooms limits the craft work and scientific exploration we can do and cramped classrooms certainly make life difficult for the teachers."

The school's active parents' association has certainly done its best. They raised £1,800 last year and have built bookshelves along one of the corridors.

"The school, with its excellent tradition for a happy working atmosphere, has a lot going for it," said Mrs Watkinson. "Despite the lack of modern facilities it is the quality of the teaching that counts, and there are no complaints about that. We are very much on view here, especially on Braintree market days, so we could not hide much from the public."

As for the solution to its problems Mrs Watkinson is not sure. "There is so much tradition bound up in this building," she said. "But what I am most worried about at the moment is that people think the school is going to close. The rumours came from Braintree Council and spread like wildfire. The message is, despite our difficulties we are doing a good job and shall continue to do so."

Eve Sweeting
Pictures by
Dave Barker

Nine-year-old Janine Humes uses the inadequate classroom sinks.

CHILDREN making the daily trek across the street to the canteen.

Photo 7.30 Braintree and Witham Times Thursday November 25, 1982 report on the rumours of closing the school.

'We're here to stay' says head

But old school has problems

IT was more than 100 years ago, in 1862, that Manor County Primary School, Braintree, first opened its doors.

And says headmistress Mrs Anne Watkinson, there is no reason why it should not carry on for a further 100 years or so.

Rumours, emanating from councillors, that the school is to close have caused a lot of anxiety among parents and staff, says Mrs Watkinson. The building may be old and inadequate but the school, with its cheerful family reputation is carrying on.

At this month's governors meeting Essex County Council firmly set fears at rest by stating: " There is no intention of closing the school."

If a replacement building is to be found then such a project would have to compete with other replacement projects with limited money available.

" The important thing," says Mrs Watkinson, who became headmistress just over a year ago, " is that people realise the school is not closing. We are here to stay."

However, there are accommodation problems — and Mrs Watkinson hopes Essex County Council will consider improvements a priority.

The five to 11-year-old children have to cross Manor Street every day to have their lunch in a temporary war-time canteen where they also have PE.

In the junior part of the school the children have to use antiquated outdoor toilets. Only one of the nine classrooms has a sink it it and two classrooms are too small for the optimum number of children.

" The school really needs tens of thousands of pounds to bring it up to date," said Mrs Watkinson. " The lack of sinks in classrooms limits the craft work and scientific exploration we can do and cramped classrooms certainly make life difficult for the teachers."

The school's parents' association raised £1,800 last year and have built bookshelves along one of the corridors.

" The school, with its excellent tradition for a happy working atmosphere, has a lot going for it," said Mrs Watkinson. " Despite the lack of modern facilities it is the quality of the teaching that counts, and there are no complaints about that."

Story: EVE SWEETING
Pictures: TONY TUNBRIDGE

• Pupils crossing Manor Street to have their lunch in a temporary war-time canteen.

• Blowing bubbles in a science lesson are Marcel McCracken, Richard Mabey and Mari Arthanasiadis, all aged ten.

Photo 7.31 Essex Braintree Chronicle Wednesday November 24, 1982 report on the rumours of closing the school.

no proper seats on the junior toilet pans, just the two wooden edges seen in photo 6.17 in the previous chapter. During the winter, the hot and cold water still frequently froze over and the toilets froze up during the day when the doors were opened for any length of time. Later adaptations enabled the staff to use a part of the infant facilities. After much lobbying, the small junior wooden seated toilet pans were replaced with more up to date ones.

In spite of repeated requests to the county council, nothing was done about this situation. In 1984, at a time when there was no caretaker, Anne was forced to unblock the drains in the boys' toilet herself. It may seem that a disproportional amount of the book is focusing on toilet issues but readers may remember from their own school days, school toilets can feature large in the minds of children from a hygiene point of view as well as the social or unsocial activities that happen there.

It was not until 1987, when the authorities finally agreed to break though from the marching corridor to the toilet area to provide access to the junior toilets from the inside of the building. The boys' urinal was finally brought into more private and safe situation away from the back wall. Photos 7.27, 7.28 & 7.29

The portaloos still were used in the playground and for the canteen across the road until closure.

Towards closure

The final blow came when public meetings were held to consult parents and the community about the possible closure. For many years the local education authority had thought privately about closing the school but it was not general knowledge. However, by the beginning of 1985 there was talk in the town of closure of the school.

David Grice said 'as a governor I was fully aware of the high esteem in which the school was held within the local community and during a painful series of meetings in company with my fellow County Councillor from Bocking, the late Peter White and education department officers, I could not help but sense the underlying anger welling up within the crowded and vociferous gatherings of anxious parents.'

The parents demanded that the school must survive, not only as a long-established school but as a focal point for the community in the central area of the town. Many of those parents had themselves been Manor Street pupils and they could not accept that the planned replacement primary school at Beckers Green would serve pupils from homes in the town centre.

But the school was not really fit for late 20th century education with its split site, busy location, cramped and some unsavoury accommodation and no nearby playing fields. Essex County

Essex County Council

EDUCATION DEPARTMENT
PO Box 47 Threadneedle House Market Road Chelmsford CM1 1LD

J O Morris MA
County Education Officer

Dear Parent

CHAPEL HILL AND MANOR COUNTY PRIMARY SCHOOLS

The site of Manor School is split on either side of a busy road. Under modern requirements, the total site is enough for only a much smaller school.   The playing field is off Courtauld Road just over a quarter of a mile away across busy main roads. There are at present no suitable alternative sites in the town centre to rebuild the school. The existing buildings are substandard, and there is very little room on the main site to extend them.

There is a significant amount of new housing in the present catchment area of Chapel Hill School, and in particular along Cressing Road. In order to accommodate these higher numbers Chapel Hill School could be extended, probably as a separate Infants and Junior School organisation on the same site, to serve the whole area. Alternatively, a second Primary School could be provided on a site set aside by the District Council to the east of Cressing Road.

Members of the Education Committee have been discussing these issues and meetings have taken place with the Governors and Headteachers of both schools to discuss how best to plan for the future.

The Governors and staff of Manor School have concluded, with regret, that the retention of the present premises is undesirable for the future needs of the children and favour moving to another site. The Governors and staff of Chapel Hill School would support either an enlarged school on the existing site or a second school in the Cressing Road area.

These consultations with the Governing Bodies at each School have led to a suggestion which has been welcomed by both, that a 'double-shift' involving the two Schools is the best way forward. Chapel Hill School suitably renamed, would transfer into premises which would be built on the site to the east of Cressing Road. Manor School would then transfer into the vacated premises at Chapel Hill, after they had been suitably enlarged and significantly improved. Both Schools would retain their present organisation, Governors, staff and children on roll at the time they move premises. Catchment areas would need to be adjusted to create two Primary Schools of about the same size - around 300 places each. Illustrative maps showing the possible effect of these proposals are attached.

In order to implement these changes, a large amount of building work would have to be planned. This means that the earliest possible date for the completion of the premises off Cressing Road would be September 1988 and Manor School would transfer to the enlarged and improved premises on Chapel Hill as soon as possible thereafter. Your views are now being sought on these proposals. Meetings for parents and other interested persons will be held as follows;

      Wednesday 26 June - Manor County Primary School at 7.30 p.m.
      Thursday 27 June - Chapel Hill County Primary School at 7.30 p.m.

If you are unable to come, and/or if you want to put your views more fully than is possible at these meetings, please write before 31 August 1985, to:-

      The Education Officer
      Area Education Office
      Crossman House
      Station Road
      Braintree CM7 6QA

Photos 7.32 The letter sent to parents about the double shift proposal

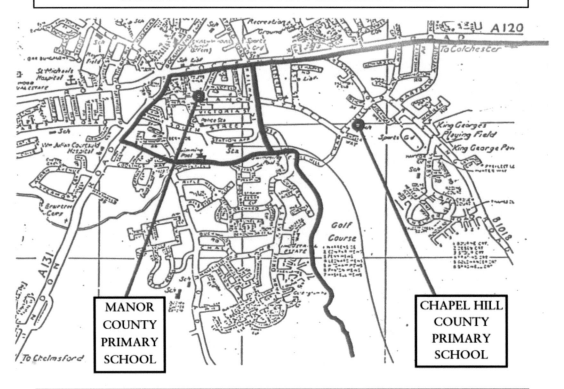

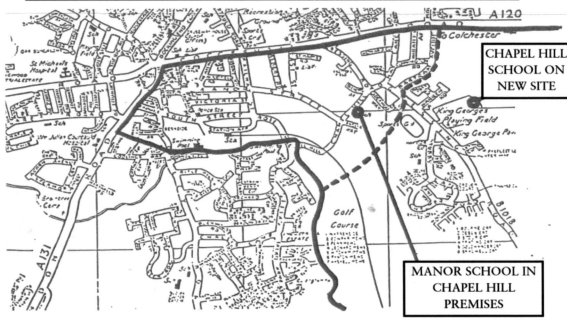

Photo 7.33 Maps of proposed catchment area changes enclosed with the letter

Essex BRAINTREE Chronicle

FRIDAY, JULY 5, 1985

Manor County Primary at Braintree.

PARENTS TOLD OF IDEA

Town schools in move plan

PLANS to move two of Braintree's oldest schools have provoked a mixed reaction.

The county council has suggested that Manor County Primary School pupils move out of their Victorian building into Chapel Hill primary, about a mile away while the Chapel Hill youngsters move into a brand new school in Cressing Road.

by SUE ROBERTS

Opposition to the idea has come from some Manor County parents who are worried about the distance their children would have to travel, the roads they would have to cross and the fact that Chapel Hill is on the edge of an industrial estate which will grow, and could create pollution.

But the chairman of the PTA, Mrs Edna Salmon is worried that too much opposition will mean nothing is done.

CRAMPED

"The amenities at the school are terrible," she said. "The children have to cross a road which is a death trap with lorries and taxis every day to get to the canteen. There's not a blade of grass on the site and conditions are cramped, although the staff do a marvellous job."

She added: "I understand why these parents are concerned, but if too much protesting is done we won't get anything and the children need something done now."

Headmistress Mrs Anne Watkinson is in favour of the move. "Something has got to be done for the children as quickly as possible," she said.

"We are on a cramped split site with our playing field a quarter of a mile away.

"I know the state of uncertainty is worrying some parents, but I want to reassure them that Manor County School will carry on as it always has."

Head of Chapel Hill Mr Ken Smale said "I think we are all in favour of the move here. We have no great worries, but at the moment everything is in limbo."

Chairman of the county education committee, Paul White, chaired parents' meetings to explain the proposals at both schools last week.

The county wants to see a new school built next to the King George V playing field in Cressing Road which would hopefully open in three years time.

Chapel Hill pupils would be moved into it and their old school extended and modernised ready for Manor County pupils.

Mr Mayn said parents have until the end of August to write in to the authority with their views which will be passed on to the education committee.

Happy youngsters at Chapel Hill Primary School this week.

Photo 7.34 Essex Braintree Chronicle 1985 report on the possible move

SCHOOLS MAY BE ON MOVE

by
VIVIENNE LOOMES

PLANS are being put forward to move two town centre Braintree primary schools to new sites — but some parents are concerned that they are only being discussed with people whose children are pupils now.

The schools are Manor County primary, whose site is split by one of the busiest roads in the town, and Chapel Hill primary, a mile away in the shadow of a large factory complex.

Essex County Council is suggesting building a new Chapel Hill school off Cressing Road, where a huge housing development is planned to take place, and refurbishing the present building so that Manor County can move into it.

County education committee chairman Paul White chaired two parents' meetings on Wednesday and Thursday to explain suggestions. They were attended by only a handful of the parents of the 300 children at both schools.

parents of the 300 children at both schools.

The county would like to see a new school adjacent to the King George V playing field opening in three years time and the existing Chapel Hill school refurbished by the 1989-90 academic year.

North West area education officer Brian Mellor says that if the moves are agreed building could start next year. Because the schools are to be moved and not closed the county can take a decision without seeking the approval of the Secretary of State.

"I think generally the governors, staff and parents are happy with the proposals but inevitably there will be some reservations and we are looking at ways of dealing with these."

He added that children living in the Godlings Way-Kentworthy Road area of the town, who

would be furthest from the new Manor County School, had the choice of attending John Ray School.

Parent Robert Worley, of Victoria Street, echoes some parents' fears when he says that everyone might be so glad of a chance to move from the problems at the existing cramped Manor County site that they will not think clearly enough about the disadvantages of the new building.

"The main problem is that Chapel Hill is in the middle of an industrial estate which will grow, especially if there is a link road to the bypass. It is an out-of-the-frying-pan-into-the-fire situation. It is also on the periphery of the catchment area which will mean a very long walk for many people — along the privately-owned Lake and Elliot road — because there is no

bus route. It will be very daunting for mothers with young children."

His neighbour Mr Kim Sherwood, who has two children at the school and a third due to start in two years' time, says that county officials give the impression that they have already taken the decision to move.

Mr Mellor said that the decision to consult only with parents whose children were already at the schools had been taken because the move — if it goes ahead — would be relatively quick.

He added that other county-owned sites in the town had been considered — off Courtauld Road on land originally scheduled for the Bradford Street bypass, in the Avenue where the Youth Training Scheme operates, and at the existing Tabor High School site in Coggeshall Road which might become vacant if that school is centralised on another site. But they were either unsuitable or not immediately available.

Concern at plan to move schools

PLANS are being put forward to move two town centre Braintree primary schools to new sites.

But some parents are concerned that the moves are only being discussed with people whose children are pupils now.

The schools are Manor County Primary, whose site is split by one of the busiest roads in the town, and Chapel Hill Primary a mile away in the shadow of a large factory complex.

Essex County Council is

suggesting building a new Chapel Hill school off Cressing Road, where a huge housing development is planned to take place, and refurbishing the present building so that Manor County can move into it.

County education committee chairman Paul White has chaired two parents' meetings to explain the suggestions.

The county would like to see a new school adjacent to the King George V playing field opening in three years' time and the existing Chapel Hill School refurbished by the 1989-90 academic year.

North west area education officer Brian Mellor says that if the moves are agreed building could start next year.

Parent Robert Worley, of Victoria Street, echoed some parents' fears when he said that everyone might be so glad of a chance to move from the problems at the existing cramped Manor County site that they will not think clearly enough about the disadvantages of the new building.

He said: "The main problem is that Chapel Hill is in the middle of an industrial estate which will grow.

Photo 7.35 Braintree and Witham Times and Evening Gazette reports on the 1985 proposals

LEA came up with a practical proposal which would not mean the closure of this popular school but a re-siting with a redrawing of school boundaries. A new school in that area of Braintree was needed so the idea was to move Chapel Hill School into the new school building at Becker's Green redrawing their catchment area to include the proposed new housing. Then, re-modelling the primary school building at Chapel Hill for the use of Manor staff and pupils with a larger catchment area including their current one. Catchment areas were much more rigidly adhered to than they are now with Free Schools and Academies out of LEA control. This move would retain the ethos, culture and staff of both schools and provide them both with up-to-date sites and buildings. Photos 7.32 & 7.33

The Governors of both schools were supportive of this idea at first. The children would have continuity and well designed, fit for purpose premises with proper playing fields attached. When the first public meeting was held it was clear that parents were not supportive of the idea and by the second public meeting held in Chapel Hill School, their Governors had changed their minds. They wanted to stay in their own building and have it remodelled around them. Manor could not continue as it was and it could not move to the new site at Becker's Green without completely changing catchment areas, thus it had to close. Then the parents started to protest at the closure. By the end of the summer term in 1985, children started to leave the school and an action group was started to try to keep the school open. This was all reported in the press. Photo 7.36 & 7.37

In the meantime, there were more problems for the school as the unions started industrial action; this was not related to the possible school closure but to the government's regulations over the hours which teachers should work, their pay and proposed new regulations over their working day. However, the unsettled state of the school future added to the teachers' insecurity. The unionised teaching staff 'withdrew their goodwill' thereby leaving the premises at lunchtime, not running any clubs, organising school visits or writing reports. Whilst this put a burden on the headteacher and support staff, the parents and pupils were largely unaware of this union action.

David Grice, governor added 'In essence, then, there was no choice other than for the head to rule the heart. For all the protracted local consultations that took place, closure was inevitable. There was no hidden agenda; the decision was based purely on educational criteria and when the final decision was made, there was a commitment to use the closure as an opportunity to provide enhanced facilities within the town centre.'

The local area ECC Education Officer, Brian Mellor, advised the head in October 1985 that the school was to be closed as soon as possible. Anne made representations that this could not have been a worse time with the union action taking place but the following spring term, Mr. Mellor advised the teaching staff at a meeting to which they had been invited that the closure would take place in 1987. Support staff had not been invited to this meeting, so another was

Parents to fight primary school move

by VIVIENNE LOOMES

A PARENTS' action committee has been set up to fight the suggested move of Braintree's Manor County primary school to the present Chapel Hill primary site.

Instead they want the 300 children and their teachers to transfer to the Coggeshall Road buildings of Tabor High when that school is centralised on one site.

And now they are canvassing for support from other parents and suggesting they send Essex County Council a protest letter putting forward the alternative proposal.

Parent Robert Worley says the four-strong action group has already found considerable support among other parents and from district and county councillors: " We are very optimistic."

TALKS

The county is suggesting building a new Chapel Hill school off Cressing Road, where a huge housing development is planned, and refurbishing the present building so Manor County can move into it.

If the moves are agreed, building could start next year and the new school could open in three years' time with Manor County moving by 1989. No plans have yet been made about centralising the split-site Tabor High although talks are taking place. Parents have until August 31 to make their views known on the Manor County-Chapel Hill move.

The parents say the Chapel Hill School is " a very unsatisfactory solution " to the problems of rehousing Manor County.

They claim the Chapel Hill area is already very industralised and it suffers severe pollution problems.

Photo 7.36 Evening Gazette July 9, 1985 report of parental action

Parents protest

AN ACTION committee has been set up by parents fighting the suggested move of the Manor County Primary School in Braintree.

They have collected more than 100 signatures from other parents who back their attempt to change the county council's mind on the move.

Education chiefs want to shift pupils into the present Chapel Hill primary site when that school moves out into a new purpose-built school in Cressing Road.

But the protesting parents want their children to be rehoused on the Tabor High site in Coggeshall Road if the comprehensive school is centralised in Panfield Lane.

Headmistress Mrs Anne Watkinson has backed the county plan because she says there is an urgent need to move pupils out of the cramped Victorian building which is on a split site with no playing field.

Action committee parent Valerie Worley commented: "We all want a new school and I know the teachers want to move for all the right motives. We are battling for the same ends.

"But I feel they are grabbing at this County Hall scheme because it is all that is on offer at the moment.

The action group claim they have the support of the majority of parents and are also canvassing district and county councillors and have contacted MP Tony Newton.

Parents main worry about the Chapel Hill plan is the fear of pollution problems from the industrial area which is due to expand and the traffic dangers which would face pupils walking to and from the school.

Mr Kim Sherwood who has two children at Manor County and one younger child of two and a half, said, "We moved from the Chapel Hill area so the children could go to Manor Street.

"There are lots of reasons why I am against the move. Traffic danger is one and the fact that it is an industrial area with a large foundry nearby. Also the school falls right on the edge of the catchment area which means around 80 per cent of pupils would have to walk through that factory area to get to school.

Mr Sherwood added, "Like the teachers I am all for a move, but to the Tabor site,

not Chapel Hill. As a parent I would rather wait a year longer so the school could move to a site which seems to have everything going for it."

The campaign has the backing of the town's Liberal county councillor David Grice. In a letter to the area education office this week he points out the traffic dangers to children if the shift to Chapel Hill goes ahead.

Mr Grice goes on to suggest that a decision on Tabor's future could be pushed through earlier allowing work on a new or expanded school to begin next year.

Then, he says, work on a new Manor School could start the following year allowing pupils to move in the autumn of 1990.

Parents have until the end of August to comment on the "double shift" porposals.

No decision has been taken on the future of Tabor High School yet, a county council spokeswoman said this week. "We are considering three alternatives," she said. "Either to house the school all at Coggeshall Road, or at Panfield Lane or to build a new school at Gypsy Corner."

Photo 7.37 Essex Chronicle Friday July 2, 1985 report of proposed parental action

Primary school 'closure' letter

A LETTER is going out to parents today about the suggested closure of Manor County Primary School in Braintree.

The letter from education chiefs puts forward the idea that places can be found for the children at other Braintree schools.

A county council spokesman said yesterday: "We have taken parents' views and the needs of the children into account. We know there was a lot of opposition last year to the idea of moving pupils into Chapel Hill School. Now members feel the best way forward is to close the school and find places for pupils in other schools."

If the plan is approved the earliest date for closure would be August next year and could well be later to fit in with the building of a new primary school in Cressing Road.

Comments will first go to the school's re-organisation and development working group. If members give closure the green light it will then be considered by the schools sub-committee and the education committee.

Last summer the county's suggestion that pupils should be moved from the cramped Victorian school in the town centre to Chapel Hill Primary about a mile away provoked a mixed reaction.

Staff and some parents were in favour of the move,

but other parents formed an action committee to fight the suggested switch.

Mr Rob Worley, a member of the action committee and a parent governor of Manor School said yesterday a substantial majority of parents were against the move and their objections had been sent to the education office.

The action committee agrees that conditions at Manor Street are not ideal with a split site, a dangerous road to cross and no playing field for the children. But they are against the Chapel Hill move because they say it would mean many pupils facing a long walk to school with traffic danger and pollution problems from the industrial area.

Photo 7.38 Essex Braintree Chronicle report on closure letter sent to parents in 1986

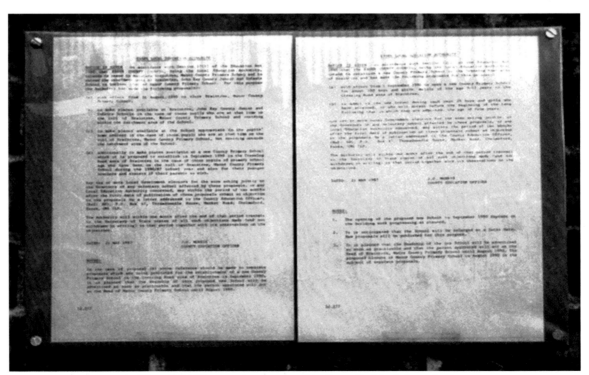

Photo 7.39 The actual notice pinned to the wall of the infant school

Photo 7.40 Braintree & Witham Thursday March 13 , 1986

Parents call for re-think on closure

by
LUCY DYSON

PROTESTING parents crowded out a hall to voice their opinions about the proposed closure of Braintree's Manor County Primary School.

Over 150 people turned up at Monday's public meeting, held in the town centre school, and questioned education officers and county councillors.

Parents urged that the catchment area of the school be looked at again, along with the possibility of transferring it to the Tabor High School site.

It was only two weeks ago that the shock news of the proposals to close the 210 pupil school were made.

Malcolm Bryan, district councillor and school governor, came to the meeting with a surprise invitation from the chairman of Braintree council, Allan Millam.

"The chairman of Braintree District Council has asked me to say that there should be a discussion for the council and the education department to look at the possibility of the Tabor site," he said.

Mr Bryan also said that the Tabor plan, of building a replacement school if the site becomes available, is worth a feasibility study.

Allan Millam explained that he would like a meeting between the district and county council

to see what their ideas are for the main schools sites in the town.

"Braintree District Council would like to see these sites and have some say in the re-development and at the moment we are fairly well in the dark about what county council is proposing for the Tabor High School and Manor County Primary School sites." he said.

"We are obviously concerned that there are so many people against the closure of Manor," he added.

He said it is far too early to talk about the possibility of any money coming from the district council.

Principal education officer, Tony Jackson said: "Braintree is going to have an increase in population and more houses, but unfortunately for this school these new houses and pupils numbers will not have a significant effect on this central part of the town."

Mr Jackson explained that the school would not come up to the standards being set in the government's new education bill, ready by 1991.

Paul White, chairman of the

county council's education committee said: "We want to spend money in Braintree and we want good schools but we can't build schools where we have not got the children."

And according to the education department figures there are only 90 children actually in Manor's catchment area which go to the school.

The county council has already agreed to the building of a new 300 place primary school in Cressing Road, designed for the developing housing estate. Work on the school is expected to start in June.

Education officers have not yet said what will happen to the pupils at Manor school but it has been thought that there are enough spaces in the town's other schools.

At the meeting parents were told that in those other schools there are 320 spare spaces.

George Warner, of Duggers Lane, Braintree, was concerned at the thought of his child going into demountable classrooms.

Mrs Valerie Worley, from South Street, Braintree, said: "I am one of the minority who lives in the catchment area. Where do I go with my children, do I drag them across an industrial estate?"

BATTLE FOR SCHOOL LOST

Closure date set for 1990

BRAINTREE'S doomed primary school will close in 1990.

County councillors are expected to rubber-stamp the closure of Manor County Primary School at a meeting next week.

The town centre school – which is celebrating its 125th anniversary – was earmarked for closure because of the falling number of pupils.

Parents immediately launched a campaign to save the school.

Despite the protests, a meeting of an education committee on Monday looks set to recommend the school closes on August 31, 1990.

BACKED

But last night plans to build a 350-place primary school in the town to serve a major housing development near the new by-pass was backed by councillors.

The £535,000 school should be completed by September, 1990 – one month after Manor County Primary closes.

by
VIVIENNE LOOMES

But there are no plans to accommodate the children from Manor County Primary in the new school near Becker's Green Road.

Instead the county council has allocated £1,330,000 to provide extra places in other town centre schools.

Last night a Braintree Council planning committee backed the new school – but wants to have another look at car parking facilities.

Photo 7.41 Evening Gazette, Wednesday, April 8, 1987

'SCHOOL TO SHUT BY 1990'

THE future of Braintree's threatened Manor Primary School looks blacker this week.

Parents who went along to a public meeting at the Victorian school on Tuesday night were told the county is now seriously considering closure by 1990.

"They really don't see any future for the school in the town centre," said parent Rob Worley who has led an action committee to fight the closure, first suggested in 1985.

"The only positive thing about this is that the county is having to look into the provision of primary school places in the town more thoroughly."

Parents had hoped the 180-pupil school, which is housed on a cramped split site in the town centre, could be moved into a new building on the "Tabor triangle" off Coggeshall Road, but the idea has failed to gain county or district council support.

Instead, pupils left at the school when it closes will be shared around other primary schools in the town.

And parents were told the county is setting aside £1.3 million to pay for those places.

They were given a guarantee that children at Manor — and their younger brothers and sisters — can go to the brand new Cressing Road school when it opens in three years' time.

The 300-pupil school is expected to cost £535,000 to build.

The majority of children from the Manor catchment area will go to John Ray primary school where a £½ million package of improvements, including three new permanent classrooms, is planned. The school should then be able to offer 90 spare places by 1990.

Expansion at White Court primary school and modernisation work at Chapel Hill make up the rest of the scheme.

A county spokesman described the meeting as "constructive". "Nobody wants to see a school die, but I think we were sympathetically received by the audience and the reasons we put for a possible closure of the school were understood," he said.

But he stressed that no final decision had been taken and no formal proposals for closure made. If parents continue to object strongly, the decision could rest finally with the Education Secretary Kenneth Baker.

Photo 7.42 Essex Chronicle Friday January 30, 1987 report on date for closure

held for them. By this time, there was uproar; the governors were highly critical of the manner in which the information had been given and over the timing of the closure without consultation. The staff and the parents were up in arms. Mr. Mellor attended a governor's meeting in February 1986 but this did not calm things down and parents continued to remove their children. The notice of closure was sent to parents in a letter home and the closure notice had to be put on the exterior wall of the infant school. Photos 7.38 & 7.39

But the protest at closure went on.

Meanwhile the school was inspected and the inspector commented that 'in spite of all the trials a great deal of progress had been made in the education of the pupils.' The final report stated that 'It is greatly to the credit of the staff that in spite of the handicaps imposed by a difficult building... upholding its reputation of purposeful industry and solid achievement.'

The positive end of the school

In the middle of all this disturbance and depressing news, the school was due to celebrate its 125th anniversary. The staff decided to make the most of the opportunity to raise morale of parents, children and themselves by having a year of activities during the academic year 1986-87 To mark this milestone. Children investigated the entries in the log books and interviewed old pupils and staff.

Three tea parties were held during the winter, one for old pupils who were retired, one for those of working age and one for children who had gone on to secondary school. Nearly a hundred people attended each one and at one point four headteachers of the school were present together – Miss Jarvis, Mrs. Want, Mr. Tyler and Anne. Photos 7.43 to 7.45

Photo 7.43 125th anniversary reunion for secondary aged ex-pupils

Photo 7.44 125th anniversary reunion for retired ex pupils

An assembly was held on the actual date in April of the anniversary of the opening ceremony, at which the then Chair of Governors helped light a model cake with 125 candles on and cut and eat a simple cake also in the shape of the school. Children had also been making a scale model of the school in their technology time. Photos 7.46 & 7.47

Reunion delight

MORE than 60 former teachers and other school staff remembered the good old days at a reunion at Manor County Primary School last week.

The school is 125-years-old next year and joining present headmistress Mrs Anne Watkinson and her staff were school heads dating from 1940.

"The best thing about the reunion was to see the delight on people's faces when they saw old friends and colleagues — often for the first time in years," said Mrs Watkinson.

Other events planned include a reunion of ex-pupils, a display of memorabilia, a picnic on sports day and a Victorian-style fete.

Photo 7.45 The Braintree and Witham Times report of the 125th anniversary meeting of four headteachers

A pageant was held at the end of the year based on extracts telling the history of the school from the log books. Some of the photos have been used already through this book. The local radio hams, using short wave radio, spent the night in the school doing a 24 hour special event trying find any contacts of the school throughout the world. Photo 7.48

A whole school photo taken at the time can be seen in the museum.

Photo 7.46 Stan Chapman, Chair of Governors at the 125th anniversary children's assembly with cake and staff lighting candles

Photo 7.47 The youngest children blowing out the 125 candles

The school went on successfully to its closure in 1990 when there were still over 80 children on roll who went with the teachers and support staff to Becker's Green. Andy Jones recalls being appointed Head of the new school at Becker's Green in 1989, when he had to oversee the closure of Manor Street. Steve Burnup was the teacher with the lower juniors, Steve Butler the top juniors and the infants were taught by Margaret Deer and Diane Rowshangohar. Although there had been quite a lot of anger Andy recalled, at the closure of Manor Street School and parents had the option of transferring their children to Becker's Green, nevertheless there remained eighty four pupils and the school successfully taught the full primary curriculum. The pupils worked well and the staff morale was high because they knew that their jobs were confirmed at Becker's Green. The school caretaker also came to the new school: he was a much loved character – John Tofts – who was very gentlemanly and proper with a wicked sense of humour. Several pupils did very well at their work during

Photo 7.48 Radio hams have an all-night vigil

125th get-togethers

ONE of Braintree's oldest primary schools is planning a series of re-unions to celebrate its 125th anniversary this year.

So if you ever sat behind a desk at Manor County Primary School — or Manor Street as it used to be known — then headmistress Anne Watkinson wants to hear from you.

The first event is a Grandparents Tea Party for all pupils who were at the school up to 1950.

That's on February 4 and will be followed on March 11 by a Parents' Tea Party for the Class of 1950 to around 1980.

A smilialr get-together will be held on March 25 for old pupils who are still at school.

Mrs Watkinson says she hopes to reach as many ex-pupils and people associated

by SUE ROBERTS

with the long history of the school as possible during the year.

She would also welcome any items of memorabilia, including photographs and people's own memories of the school.

She hopes to publish a small booklet about the history of the school and with descriptions of school life past and present by the end of the year.

● The Victorian school in the town centre is under threat of closure by the county council because of its cramped site. But parents and teachers who protested when the county plan was announced have been told this week the earliest possible date for closure now is 1990.

Preparing to celebrate — chirpy youngsters from Braintree's Manor County Primary School.

Photo 7.49 The Essex Chronicle report of the 125th anniversary reunions

this last year; some sat the 11 plus successfully and those who had specific needs were helped by a teaching assistant, Val White, who also went to the new school. Andrea Talmage, previously a welfare assistant at Manor became the new school secretary.

Over the year, of course, the empty classrooms collected a lot of dust and spiders: all the work of sorting out the equipment and furniture which was to go to the new school was done by the staff. The parents association organised a celebration for the closure and there was a sense of excitement among the pupils and staff for the new school had lovely classrooms and a field. By the time of the last day, a calm atmosphere prevailed. The log book records found for us by ERO staff tell of a 'Final performance based on items of school history before an appreciative audience of 180 parents, governors, ex-pupils and ex-staff, a fitting tribute to school's 128 years' 05.07.90. 'Final day in Manor's long history as a school. Presentations made to departing staff, scrolls presented to all children. Beautiful cake in shape of Manor School was cut. Over 100 adults attended assembly including parents, governor and ex-members of staff.' 13.07.90

'Transfer of equipment to new school Beckers Green.' 16-20.07.90

Don Parker, then head of property management at Crossmann House the Area Education Office and at the time of interview, a project manager at Essex County Hall, remembered the transport of the furniture to the new school in the yellow minivans known as Wells Fargo. Andy remembered that even the piano went. Don had sent out a memo to the other local schools to offer any surplus furniture to them. He said 'they descended like vultures' and the school was cleared in a few hours. A skip had been placed in School Lane behind the school to take the final remnants but even these disappeared overnight!

END NOTES

[1] Cockroft, 1981

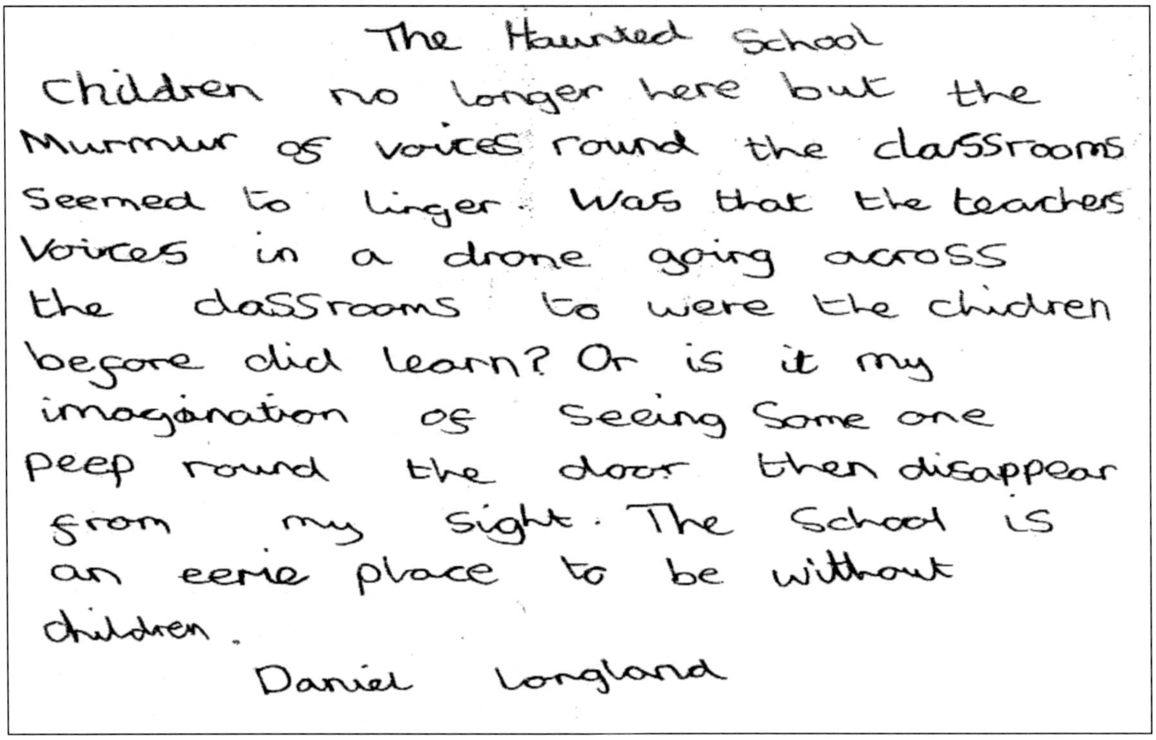

> The Haunted School
> Children no longer here but the Murmur of voices round the classrooms Seemed to linger. Was that the teachers Voices in a drone going across the classrooms to were the children before did learn? Or is it my imagination of seeing Some one peep round the door then disappear from my sight. The School is an eerie place to be without children.
> Daniel Longland

Photo 7.50 A pupil's thoughts in 1987 about the closure.

Chapter 8 Braintree District Museum

The closure of the school left the community with a centrally placed, sturdy building now empty but with very specific trust deeds. Jean Grice played a large part in the development of the new Braintree District Museum and has written a long account of the transition to the museum which now uses the building. Her account is in the museum archives but has formed the basis of this chapter. She had a background in textiles and had been instrumental in saving the Warner mills in South Street as a Working Silk Museum. Her husband, David Grice, also a governor at the school and an Essex County Councillor for the Braintree WestDivision for twelve years recalled 'a genuine sadness in having to participate in the closure of Manor Street Primary School.' At that time, the most pressing need from the County's perspective was for a new library and it was decided to investigate the use of Manor Street School for this purpose. Braintree District Council meanwhile was in the throes of investigating an ambitious plan to build a theatre, an underground car park plus a shopping and hotel complex behind the now Grade II-listed Town Hall Centre. Jean has said that during the two academic years between 1989 and 1991 after the school's closure, Braintree College took over the management of the site and gave the steering group much needed breathing space to firm up the museum proposals and put together the legal framework which could, finally after 62 years, ensure the creation of a permanent museum.

Jean recalls that county officers, though, were astounded to discover that any development of the Victorian school buildings on the north side of Manor Street was, in fact, legally restricted by the original covenants put in place by the Courtauld family. Those buildings could be only be used for educational purposes in perpetuity; specifically, its use as a library was not legally possible. Braintree's new library was located instead on Fairfield Road, leaving Manor Street School to be found a different future while still retaining its original educational function.

During this period, a steering committee was set up consisting of representatives from all the local organisations which could benefit from the proposed museum, not least Braintree District Council which would have its stored collection displayed and cared for, Essex County Council would use it for educational purposes, Brain Valley Archaeological Society could have a repository for finds from its own and the County Council's excavations. Braintree District Council would also have space for their art exhibitions and those from the thriving arts courses at the local college. Warner's, Courtauld's and Crittall's would also have somewhere public to demonstrate their historic industrial significance. It had even been proposed in 1948 that Braintree should house a museum of Textile History. Braintree Heritage Trust had been set up in 1981 and cared for a small collection housed, up to then, in the Town Hall Centre. The John Ray Trust would have a home for its original and valuable books purchased in 1986 as well as a focus for its educational work.

On the day of the civic celebrations in April 1986, when the children of Manor Street School had dressed up in 17th century costume to celebrate the life of Braintree's most celebrated son, the scientist John Ray, in a spontaneous and now very poignant gesture, Charles Daybell, Braintree District Council's chief executive, invited all the 250 or so children, teachers and helpers into the Town Hall Centre to join the 200 civic guests for the formal celebration of the 300th anniversary. Photo 8.1 Photographs of that day and the children crowded around Dr Bellamy can still be seen in the museum's John Ray Gallery. That day led to the creation of the John Ray Trust, chaired by Malcolm Bryan and also acted as a further spur to seek a new permanent home for the collection then languishing in the

Photo 8.1 Children in costume outside the Town Hall on John Ray day 1986

Town Hall Centre basement. It also brought Braintree's heritage to the attention of the councillors, not only its importance to the community at large but to its schools and colleges in particular. It also opened up the potential for promoting the Braintree area as a tourist destination and indeed the district's first tourism assistants were appointed during that year of celebration.

The Braintree District Museum Trust was consequently set up in 1991, exactly ten years after the Heritage Trust came into existence and the following year was dedicated to fund-raising; script writing; choosing the design firm and the building contractors, W P Harris. A controversy arose over the question of charging for admission, as recommended by Adrian Babbage then chair of the East Midlands Museums Federation and one of the many key

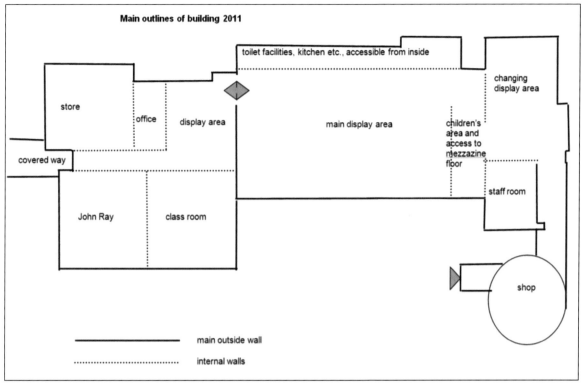

Fig 8.1 Plan of school with Museum extensions

professionals who offered advice freely in order to get the museum up and running. Again, it was education provision that decided the direction the museum was to take.

During 1991, Stephen Douglass and Jean Grice asked every school in Essex what they would like to see and do at the museum. What curriculum areas should they cover? Would they be happy to pay? What public facilities would they most want? The virtually unanimous feedback was that schools would be prepared to pay if what was on offer 'met their learning needs.' It was this survey which was later used as a model by Deborah Boden, the first Museums Development officer appointed by ECC, to influence the working relationship between museums and schools and crucially gave key direction for Braintree's embryonic museum; a future reflecting a successful past as a happy place dedicated to learning at the heart of the community.

£410,000 of funding was needed to transform the Manor Street buildings from school to museum but with one classroom left as it might have been in 1893. It was actually one in the 1911 extension. This was to remain forever as a reminder of its original purpose of the building. The funding was secured with the help of Braintree District Council and then £360,000 was allocated by the Heritage Lottery Fund towards the conversion of the former infants' building into the present Learning for Life Centre and café, which opened in November 2002. The old infant building, as the Learning for life Centre, also proved the right size to house a mural of the history of the Courtauld family.

At the opening of Braintree District Museum on October 31st, 1993 more than 400 people attended the opening ceremony that evening and over that first weekend more than 1,000 people crossed the threshold to view the transformed school. All had played some part either through fundraising, providing objects for the museum collection, or lending their time and expertise voluntarily or professionally to the project.

The museum's development is inextricably linked to the Courtauld family. Purpose-built showcases were filled with ceramics from the Courtauld family's collection together with social history oddities collected by Bocking End solicitor and antiquarian Alfred Hills; their donation was the foundation of the current collection. This historic, documented collection, although relatively small, proved

Photo 8.2 Re-enactment of a WW2 Lesson

crucial to the later stages of the fund-raising process, which in turn was dependent on the existence of a 'registered' collection. Displays in the present museum explain how the Braintree area played a unique role in Britain's industrial development, particular in the field of textiles. More importantly, the museum established

links with all the surrounding schools and were bowled over by the work produced for the schools' exhibition.

Di Naylor, who contributed towards the writing of this book, took groups of secondary school pupils to the Museum to experience life in a Victorian school. The pupils from Sible Hedingham were studying Victorian education for their GCSE and it was a unique opportunity for them to experience what it was like in a 19th century classroom. They had already studied what local schools were like in the 19th century using log books and contemporary accounts but

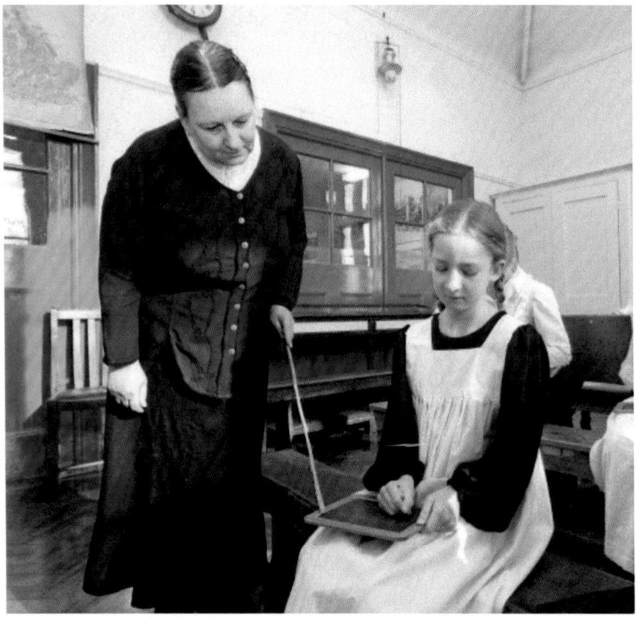

Photo 8.3 Re-enacting a Victorian lesson.

nothing prepared them for what to all intents and purposes was the real thing. Arriving at the school, they were greeted by a stern Victorian school ma'am dressed in grey flannel holding a cane in her hand. Having trooped silently into the classroom, they sat at raked desks with a slate in front of them in the classroom done up as it would have been in 1860 with a globe and charts on the wall exhorting the pupils to be good together with hymns and prayers for their souls. Valiantly, the pupils tried to do copperplate script using scratchy graphite pencils and one of them on one occasion ended up in the corner with a dunce's cap on. They chanted in rote and tried to do their sums. After a short time, one of the pupils was so scared that he suffered an asthma attack and had to be removed. After the hour-long lesson, they trooped out and said to Di 'Cor miss, I'm glad we didn't have to go to school in them days!' A salutary lesson.

We owe much to all who enabled the museum to come into being and countless children of all ages will have experienced 'living history' as well as the glass cases of artefacts, photographs and displays so well laid out.

Given the economic climate of the country following the financial problems since 2007, it is to everybody's staff, volunteers and visitors credit that the museum is still open and looking forward to a future role in central Braintree.

Chapter 9 Lessons from the past

Apart from describing, as best we can from the available evidence, what took place in the life of Manor Street School, there are themes which have permeated the story. The social history of the time it was open is clearly reflected in activities of the school. The changing education ideas and needs of the children also comes through. The log books are the foundation on which the story is built and it is sad that this is no longer a requirement of headteachers. Will the histories of schools active now be as easy to research? There is a lot of extraneous information in them but the books provided such a wealth of stories of real people and families.

The story covers a large proportion of the Victorian era, recounting the act of benevolence which established the school by a local factory owner and reflects the changing clientele of the school during the growing prosperity of the town. While established for the poorer classes, none of the children in the photographs of the later nineteenth century is without shoes, or in rags as the earlier description indicated.

The two world wars of the twentieth century saw bombs being dropped on the town, air raid warnings and air raid shelters recorded; staff were called up, even killed, children formed cadet corps; evacuee children occupied part of the school. The general depression between the wars prevented increases in salary. The increased living standards following the second world war brought the lack of appropriate toilet facilities more to the fore. There is mention throughout of holidays for pea picking, blackberry picking and other harvest pursuits. The dates of these persist in our school holiday period in August despite the fact that children rarely help with any harvests now except perhaps in their own school garden.

Interest in education, for everyone to be able to read and write, increased during Victoria's reign, ending with the establishment of compulsory education. However, it was not until the second half of the twentieth century that all children, even preschool, including those thought uneducable for medical reasons, became the responsibility of the state education system.

Governance

The school was run firstly by a committee and later a board. Local people and parents were to be involved in the running from an early stage and ladies were included, although more for the welfare and creative arts than the 'harder' aspects of school life. Again the constitution of governing bodies was not detailed in law until later in the twentieth century. The ethos established by the founding family was well before its time and proved long lasting.

Inspection was around from the beginning, without it there was no grant. It was based on attendance and the results of simple tests given by the inspectors who visited annually. Local inspection in the early days was by members of the Courtauld family. The later boards micromanaged the school and the heads of the time were little more than the everyday managers. In the first half of the last century, heads became more professionalised and had increasing freedom to lead their schools how they wished. They did not have control of the budget as they now have but were 'headteachers', involved in teaching and learning, as the name really implies.

The more market orientated political stance taken in the second half the century, assisted later by the number crunching possibilities opened up by computers, meant a much more bureaucratic oversight. After the Manor Street School closed, inspection was by Ofsted and there has been much increased central direction by central government. Local Education Authorities now largely have responsibility for channelling government funding according to national formulae and few have any advisory services.

Matthew Arnold is reputed to have said 'Payment by results would lead to cutbacks which would lower standards. The proposal treated school as a mere machine for teaching rather than a living whole with complex functions, religious, moral and intellectual.' Early Ofsted inspections tried to look at all these aspects but results of tests have again become paramount in providing information for inspection and thus for the media and parents.

Manor Street School underwent a radical change in 1938 when the all-age school became a junior mixed school with the infant school retaining its character. Then in 1952 the amalgamation of the infant and junior schools under one head took place, although the separate sites still meant an effective segregation of staff until very late on. The effect was felt in the school of all the Education Acts, particularly those of 1870, 1902, 1944 and 1986. The content the Hadow report of 1926, the Plowden report of 1967 and that of Cockcroft in 1981 were all influential on the nature of what went on in the school, as were the results of research into how children learn and ways of teaching published in the last century.

Staffing

With a few exceptions where a weak teacher is recognised or problems are mentioned, a theme of benevolence, quality of purpose and non-sectarian liberalism permeates the story. The school may have been intended for children of poorer people but the philosophy of teaching and learning professed by the staff was one of high expectations allied with care and understanding. The school was a way of life for most of the teachers, they were intensely loyal. Teacher training and professional development changes during the existence of the school; the availability of training and courses enabled teachers to continue to grow in their understanding and renew ideas.

Women made up the bulk of the teaching force and still do and yet the majority of headteachers were and are male. Manor however had its fair share of female heads. Female teachers were not supposed to continue if they got married but they seemed to be able to continue here before the law was changed. Sadly there is rarely any mention of support staff. They must have been there from the early days; a caretaker and cleaner must have existed and later secretaries and welfare helpers. With the canteen came kitchen staff.

Children and their families

Children are only mentioned by name in exceptional circumstances. Their behaviour shows little change over the years, despite the fear that children are worse behaved, or there is a moral lassitude now, etc. The log books detail incidents of theft, bullying, swearing, even muddy boots all too familiar to teachers of today. 'Boys with nothing to do are difficult to keep quiet' was noted, even in 1863.

There are a couple of break-ins, complaints about one or two families and even a punch-up which the head had to sort out. It all sounds rather familiar when reading the accounts.

Parental involvement was part of this story from the beginning although it is a much more recent phenomenon in many schools. Even in 1863 newsletters were sent home. Open days are mentioned in 1899. Parental involvement as voluntary support in classes started late in the school's history but Friends of Manor School were supportive from early days after the second world war.

The intake was firstly from the poorer classes but later seen as very mixed, both in family circumstances and learning capability. There were always children with learning problems although we now find the language then used a bit offensive e.g. 'defective.' There were always some high fliers, who later went to grammar school and/or university. Sometimes classes were streamed, sometimes children were 'set' in groups within a class.

Curriculum – the subject matter: formal, informal and hidden

The school was established as non-sectarian, unusual in its day. It had a strong Christian ethic however, which continued in various ways throughout its life. Indeed, the first head, John Saunders, left the school to go into the ministry and John Tyler, head from 1973-1981, had a year's sabbatical to take a degree in divinity. The first formal prospectus in 1984 included the words, agreed and supported by all the teaching staff to cover their views, whatever they were, atheist or ardent churchgoer: 'While there is no explicit religious bias to the school, there is little disagreement that living by the precepts of the Christian tradition will improve our attitudes to each other and the world outside.'

The Victorian era Standards gave a good outline of what should be taught at each stage – not age. They were the national curriculum of the time. Schools set their own schemes of work to deliver these Standards which were then examined. Maybe something as simple as this was the original intention of our National Curriculum which became so content heavy. Testing stopped in 1896, with payment by results finishing in 1897. However, this lack of testing was short lived, in 1907 free places in grammar schools became available as the result of tests. All schools took them. As Binet introduced his intelligence test in 1905, the era of intrinsic tests to determine ability and capability had begun.

The new set of regulations published in 1904 said that the purpose of elementary school was to fit children practically and intellectually to the work of life, to help them reach their potential and become upright and useful members of the community. It was a full curriculum in subject terms, with music, PE and physical sciences, object lessons. It was down to the ingenuity, understanding and sensitivity of the teacher to find what interested and inspired their children.

We now have the system which seems to indicate it is only for lack of teaching, or perseverance on the part of the pupil, which stops all children from passing the appropriate number of examinations or tests at various stages of their life. The earlier headteachers of Manor Street School knew that not all would reach Standard VIII level and were able to teach woodwork, cooking, needlework and other skills to enable all the pupils to lead practical and useful lives.

There were lots of extra curricular activities, entertainments and outings from the early days, a magic lantern show at Christmas 1863 and a trip to London 1876 for instance.

Pedagogy – the teaching and learning methods

The vision outlined in the opening ceremony was followed in spirit for the rest of the school's life: 'we will educate them – draw out, that is the power of their minds; we teach them to think and supply them with subjects for thought and more than this if you send your children to our school we trust and believe you will find there a good wholesome tone of truth and honour and probity.'

In 1878 the head commented that 'too much telling not enough educing, was too much like preaching.' The 1984 prospectus stated '... our main aim, as an educational establishment is to educate the children who come to us, that is to enable learning to take place, by the best means available, within the resources available to us. We are a happy and caring school and rightly proud of our reputation as such. Despite the drawbacks of an old and awkward building, we do try to provide a safe and comfortable place.'

Miss Jarvis, in 1962, described the classroom:

'Instead of rows of children chanting monotonous sounds and words, busy boys and girls will be found grouped round tables, reading from interesting, illustrated story books in the class libraries. The teacher will be moving among the children, giving individual help wherever possible.'

The move towards freedom and purported professionalism of teachers has gone back to the imposed central bureaucracy of today in the name of freedom of choice and market forces.

Equipment has gone from ball frames to computers, from slates to pen and ink and chalk and now to tablets, laptops and interactive whiteboards. The magic lantern gave way to radio, then TV and video recorders. Since the school closure this has all moved on again to the internet, search engines, smart phones and electronic communication with parents. Rows of children in galleries gave way to desks then to chairs and tables; the large hall was divided up into individual classrooms. While lecture and individual tuition maybe the way in universities, it has never caught on in primary schools and individual classrooms seem well entrenched. Even many of the revolutionary open-plan schools of the mid to late 20th century have closed off their spaces to allow direct teaching in class groups.

Health

Smallpox was still around in 1866 despite vaccination; measles is still around now despite MMR vaccine, *mumps, measles and rubella* . Whooping cough, scarlet fever and influenza were mentioned as problems for families well on into the twentieth century. There were no antibiotics until after the second world war, the school had to fumigate and disinfect to keep down bacterial infections from spreading in the crowded conditions of the school. Headlice are still a problem, not solved by chemicals or even good hygiene, they are just very successful creatures in adapting to their particular biological niche.

The log books mention milk distribution to help with malnutrition and school meals provision, including of course the building of a canteen, after the second world war.

186

Health education is mentioned from time to time including special talks on things like the dangers of alcohol. Sex education was taught through television programmes as they became available but no great issue seems to have been made of it as in some schools.

The building itself and its site

The building, while praised so highly at its opening was a difficult one from the beginning. Ventilation and heating of such a space was a trial. Part of the ceiling even fell down in 1881 from the damp. Overcrowding, due to the popularity of the school, up to 600 3 to 14 year olds on site at some periods , was a problem until the threat of closure drove some families away. Even then, over 80 children stayed on to the final closure and either went on to secondary schools or transferred with the then staff to the new school at Beckers Green. Outdoor sanitation, lack of playground and playing field space and natural resources all proved problems difficult to overcome and these, together with a site split by a busy town centre road, were the cause of closure.

The toilet provision was ever a source of worry: frost in the winter and flooding; and later as general standards rose, a real sense of disgust emanated from both children and staff. Lack of a separated head's office and staffroom catering facilities were not insurmountable but were certainly very inconvenient at times throughout the latter years.

The nearby markets, earlier the cattle market and always the main market, were noticeable in the school by smell and noise. In the later years, stalls were even under the windows of the infant building. Taxis became a source of nuisance when motorised vehicles became the norm and the long running battle between the school and the council over the problem was only resolved at the closure of the school. The 1984 prospectus stated 'We have to put a higher emphasis on road safety than most schools, as we have a split site and we have fewer creature comforts than many more modern establishments, we do have to work hard to make the building look attractive and provide extra resources, particularly natural ones, which other schools take for granted.'

There were missed opportunities of acquiring land behind the school where the Catholic Church and Sainsbury's now are but had it been acquired, it would now probably be seen as too valuable to keep. Many schools have sold part of their playing fields for development to acquire more funds since the onset of local management in schools.

When new schools were built in the town after the second world war, families still sent their children to the town centre school rather than the nearby ones, some for convenience and others seeking what they saw as a more traditional school for their offspring – despite the clear adherence by the staff to the then modern approaches of more creativity and science. Most schools are closed because the numbers of children drop as populations settle or they have such poor standards the only way to progress is to start again. This was not so for Manor

Street School. The practical difficulties of the building along with external town reviews undertaken by the county and district councils proved the death knell. The ways of doing the closure left a lot to be desired for staff, children and parents but maybe there is no right way.

Braintree continues to grow; the current use of the building by the local museum has brought another life to the building which is still an architectural focal point in the town centre. It has been a great success. It has been hit as most institutions, by the recession since 2007, both in funding and numbers of visitors but it is always developing new ways to tell the story of Braintree. We wish it well.

Appendix 1

Sources used

The main source for the material given in this book was the log books kept by the headteachers of the school. The keeping of a log book by headteachers was a requirement of the revised Code of 1862. It continued until the 1990s. These are now kept in The Essex Record Office and are available to be read by the public. However, an embargo on texts which refer to people was imposed on them, firstly for thirty years and when we came to check references for the closure period, the embargo had been extended to 100 years. This meant that the last three log books of the school were unavailable at the time of the writing and publication but will become available in later years. Thus, confidentiality is maintained. Staff of the ERO will answer direct questions on these later ones but the books cannot be examined. We had to make do with memories for these years. The log books were the basis of Miss Jarvis's, the headteacher at the time, centenary booklet and the 125th anniversary pageant. The reference numbers for these are in the bibliography.

Admission registers were also kept as well as the log books and separate punishment books. These record the date of entry of a child to the school and their date of leaving. As children are not categorised by age on the date of entry they do not provide easy sources of general information about school life.

Also in the ERO are the minutes of the school board of managers from when the school became a board school. This was a joint board in the early days so several schools' details are recorded. These tend to be more meticulously kept than the log books but sometimes sparse in detail. Again, the last years of records could not be examined.

Original documents such as deeds also exist, both in the Braintree Museum and the ERO. The museum collection of archive photographs and some sketches proved useful in trying to piece together the actual siting of buildings. Plans were not often kept until more recently. The old Ordnance Survey maps gave some information about siting and layout. These are also held in the Essex Record Office. Even though the log books were unavailable for the last ten years of the school's life, newspaper cuttings held by the museum and personal accounts have enabled us to track and date particular events around the closure.

Some background information about the school has been gleaned from accounts of the Courtauld family whose benevolence and generosity created the possibility of the school in the first place. Again, where used, these are referenced.

The knowledge and experience of the authors as trained teachers and researchers, with historical and medical backgrounds, backed up with the various texts named in the bibliography, provided the background historical, medical and educational information for the text.

Many of the recent photographs were taken by Anne while she was the headteacher. All photographs of people and children were taken at a time when permission of the subject did not have to be sought and all are at least 30 years old now. The originals are lodged in the Braintree Museum archive and references to the catalogue number is given later in these appendices. We trust no one is worried by a photograph taken when they were younger appearing in the book; actually we hope they will be pleased!

The 125th anniversary celebrations encouraged people at that time to bring in memorabilia and a few wrote accounts of their time at the school. These have proved of great interest 30 years later, including the account the children themselves wrote at the time for the BBC Domesday project, referred to in chapter 7. A day was held in February 2011, the 150th anniversary, again inviting people to contribute memories. Many photos and other items were brought in, some donated to the museum. The meeting of old friends on these occasions was very moving. The accounts given to us in that day and subsequently have been given to the museum for others to use. Some visitors to the museum have also contributed memories. The oral accounts given to Di have proved invaluable to give us a real feel of what life was like in the school. Notes taken from the meetings and some audio records are available in the museum. The actual publication of the book may also elicit further accounts and information which will be of interest to later generations. We hope so.

Lastly, it being the twenty first century, the internet has proved invaluable. Just typing some of the names from the log books of equipment used or events, artefacts or people like Matthew Arnold, one can be almost overwhelmed with ancillary data. Some of the photographs used came from the internet and are acknowledged. Emails to organisations like the Royal Institute of British Architects made it easy to access other relevant records where available. We have even tried to make contact with interested people through Facebook but our lack of familiarity with such means of communication has meant we made less use of it than is possible – perhaps someone will carry this on?

We hope that people will read our account with interest and add to it.

Appendix 2
Some dates and data

We were often asked 'how many children passed through the school?' but it is virtually impossible to tell. The headteachers either didn't record a number at all or often recorded numbers present, or average for the week or percentage of numbers on roll. It was this sort of number which was counted for 'payment by results.' One of the tasks of the inspectors, either managers or national was to check the registers to see that the heads were not cheating. Admission registers exist but they only show when the child entered or left the school not the number there at any one time. Heads also recorded the information on different days and frequently gave reasons for poor attendance – weather, events etc. Numbers on roll NOR , the number now recorded, also varied where given, as children came and went at any time of the year. Up to late in the 19th century attendance was not compulsory anyway. Now schools have to account for NOR at a particular time on a particular day each year. But, even now, accounting for leaving and entering means total numbers of individuals over any period would be difficult to calculate.

What follows here is not very accurate. The numbers were recorded at different times of the year. What it does give us, is a feel for the popularity of the school and what we would now consider gross overcrowding. Children clearly could not move about a room very much with fifty plus children in a class. Also, up to 1938, large young people up to 14 years old were also part of the total! By modern standards the school was full in 1981 with nine classes and 30ish in each class, that is about 270. When the three partitions were in place, using the canteen or moving the partitions for assemblies, three more classes were possible making 360 a full school. You can see the effect on numbers of the new schools opening in the town but the continually growing population of Braintree and continued popularity of the school meant numbers stayed up. They did not really fall until the closure possibilities were made public knowledge.

Year	Jun NOR	Junior Head	Inf NOR	Infant Mistress	Total NOR	Local Events	National events
1849						George Courtauld II started to buy land in the area	
1851						School on site	
1861						New school built – George Courtauld II died	
1862						Official opening of new building	
1863	207	John Saunders	70	Maria Gatwick	277		Victoria
1864			70	Helen Brooker			
1866			100	Eliza Wicks ('girl') after a gap. School under the Masters's care			
1868	180	G. Matthews					
1871				Infants to be run separately again			
1873			44	Elizabeth Babbington			
1875			69	Edith Castell			
1880			141	Ellen Hagben			
1881			104	Jane Miller/ Maria Unwin/E. Clark			
1882	268	R.N. Davies	92		368		
1885	249		119		368		
1889	295		144	Alice Gray	439		
1895	370		165		535	Critall's factory opened	
1897			157			New infant building	
1901							Edward VII
1906			145			Lake and Elliot's foundry opened	
1910	315		161		476		George V
1911			144			New junior extension built	
1913	383	Death Mr. Davies - Miss Hemmings then Harry Evans	128		511		
1914	376		167		543		WW1
1915	372		163		535		WW1
1916	375		156		531		WW1
1919	380	Ernest Quick	195		575		
1920	402		165		567		
1922	327			Miss Sharman		Bocking Place School opened	
1929	398					Chapel Hill School opened	
1933	400		150		550		
1936	406	Mr Lucas (County Unattached)	160		566		Edward VIII

1937	415		155					George VI
1938	245						End of Senior School	
1939		Mr. Hoare						WW2
1940		Sylvia Jarvis					Evacuees at the school	WW2
1941	253							WW2
1942	242							WW2
1943	223							WW2
1944	214							WW2
1945	241		178		419			WW2
1946	254		172		426			
1947	257							
1948	274						Canteen opened	
1949	266		188		454			
1950	279		203		482			
1951	278		202	Miss Sharman retired	480			
1952	310		171		481		Amalgamation	Elizabeth II
1953					479		John Bunyan School opened	
1955					382			
1960					353			
1962					371		Centenary	
1963					406			
1964					422			
1965		Phyllis Want			284		John Ray School opened	
1966					316			
1967					328			
1971							Great Bradfords School opened	
1973		John Tyler						
1976		Eric Broad (acting)						
1977		John Tyler						
1981		Anne Watkinson			250+			
1987		Julie Smith (County Unattached)			125			
1989		Andy Jones						
1990					80		School closes	

Appendix 3

Names of the school

In the text we have mainly used the short form of 'Manor' as that was how we the staff and LEA at my time always referred to it although locally it was often known as 'Manor Street' or 'Manor Street School.' An 1861 deed refers to the 'old building known as Manor Road School' having already been conveyed to the trustee group.

In 1862, at the opening ceremony, George Courtauld the younger is reported to have said 'For some years past a considerable school has been conducted on these premises called Manor Road School or The Public Training School or Mr Rees's School.'

The school has had various names over the years, firstly known as the Braintree Public Schools infant and mixed at the opening in 1862.

The log books rarely refer to their own name, although in 1887, Manor Street Mixed School is mentioned.

The managers' minutes refer to the pair infant and junior as Braintree Council School as distinct from the ones in Bocking and Manor Street Mixed and Infants in 1903.

In 1912, they write it as Braintree Manor Street Council School.

In 1938, when the older children leave, the main school becomes Braintree Manor Street County Junior School and the infant school Braintree Manor Street County Infant School.

In 1952, on amalgamation, it becomes Braintree Manor Street County School.

By 1859 it is renamed Braintree Manor County Primary School.

In 1981, it was officially known as Manor County Primary School, Braintree.

Text quotes

Those with an asterisk before them are useful texts for the general reader interested in further reading

ANON. 1862. The opening ceremony of Manor School. Braintree and Bocking Advertiser 1862 Essex Record Office E/Z 44/2

ARCHIVES. 1846-1918. Halstead Literary and Mechanics Institute [Online]. Chelmsford: Seax - Essex Archives Online; Essex Record Office. [Accessed December 2009].

*BAKER, M. 1981. The book of Braintree and Bocking, Buckinghamshire, Barracuda books Ltd.

BALL, N. 1893. A documentary history of elementary schools in England 1840-1870, London, Maurice Temple Smith.

BARDELL, M. 1996. A sense of place: The origin of Braintree and Bocking street names, Braintree, Bardell, M.

BBC. 2010. Local history - Fact files [Online]. London: bbc.co.uk/history.

BETTLEY, J. & PEVSNER, N. 2007. *Essex,* New Haven and London, Yale University Press.

BRADHURST. Microfilm of Documents of Bradhurst family of Rivenhall Place [Online]. Chelmsford, Essex: Essex Record Office. [Found on web 11.10.09].

BULLOCK, A. 1975. A language for life. London: DES and HMSO.

COCKROFT, W. H. 1981. Mathematics Counts. London: HMSO.

COLEMAN, D. C. 1969. *Courtaulds: An economic and social history,* London, Oxford Unversity Press.

CUNNINGHAM, P. 2002. Primary Education. In: ALDRICH, R. ed. A century of education. London and New York: Routledge Falmer.

*CURTIS, S. J. 1967. History of Education in Great Britain, London, University Tutorial Press.

GARDNER, P. 2002. Teachers. In: ALDRICH, R. ed. A century of education. London and New York: Routledge Falmer.

GOSDEN, P. 1989. The department and governance of the system. 1839-1989 Public Education in England 150th Anniversary. London: Department of Education and Science and Her Majesty's inspectorate of Schools.

JARVIS, S. 1962. A history of Manor County Primary School, Braintree, Manor County Primary School.

LAWRENCE, H. 2009. Measuring worth: Purchasing power of British pounds from 1264 to present. internet: URL http://www.measuringworth.com/ppoweruk/.

MARTIN, G. 2004. A brief history of state intervention in British schooling. In: MATHESON, D. ed. An introduction to the study of education. 2nd ed. London: David Fulton Publishers.

*PLOWDEN, B. 1967. Children and their primary schools. A report of the Central Advisory Council for Education England . London: HMSO.

*QUIN, W. 1981. History of Braintree and Bocking, Lavenham, Suffolk, Lavenham Press Ltd.

ROWLEY, N. ed. 1974. Education in Essex No.6, Chelmsford: Essex Record Office.

SILVER, P. & SILVER, H. 1974. The education of the poor, London and Boston, Routledge & Kegan Paul Ltd.

SMITH, P. W. 1987. ref Visit to Manor St School on 4-2-1987. Letter. Braintree: Braintree museum.

SPEED, P. F. 1964. Learning and teaching in Victorian times, Harlow, Longman.

WIKIPEDIA. 2010. Elementary Education Act 1870 [Online]. Wikipedia. [Accessed 18.11.10]

List of Photographs

Key To References

ERO   Essex Record Office

BRNTM   Braintree Museum

AW   Anne Watkinson

Cover	The Early Infant School	BRNTM	2325
P1.1	The earliest known image of the building 1864	BRNTM	?
P1.2	The town centre of Braintree in 1844 from the deeds of Hyde Farm	ERO	D/DO/V T31
P1.3	Lots along Manor Street to be sold in 1853 from deeds of Hyde Farm	ERO	D / D O / T31
P1.4	Part of the 1848 conveyance	BRNTM	?
P1.5	Part of the 1849 conveyance	BRNTM	?
P1.6	Map of site of Chapel Field from 1863	ERO	D/DO/Q 9/23
P1.7	Bell in use in 1980 and the original old bell from the steeple	BRNTM	1994/18 0/43
P1.8	East gable end of the building showing the site of the original foundation stone under the window, now rendered over	AW	
P1.9	Title page of first infant log book	ERO	E / M L 193/1
P1.10	The start of the cutting from the Braintree Advertiser 16.04.62. Added date incorrect	ERO	E/Z 44/2
Fig 1.1	Map showing location of Braintree	AW	
P2.1	Newspaper cuttings mounted on hardboard reporting opening ceremony, Braintree and Bocking Times 16.4.1862	ERO	E/Z 44/2
P2.2	Donor of cuttings also on hardboard	ERO	E/Z 44/2
P2.3	Start of first cutting from Braintree and Bocking Times 16.04.1862	ERO	E/Z 44/2
P2.4	1987, scene from pageant rehersal of children re-enacting the opening ceremony	BRNTM	1994.18

P2.5	Map of two buildings shown on map of auctioneer's details for the sale of Mount House Estate	ERO	D/DO T31
P2.6	Braintree Institute, Bocking End	BRNTM	2024
P2.7	Stone version of trust deed in main room	BRNTM	1994/17 6.13
P2.8	Feed my lambs, on gable end of building	AW	
P2.9	Plan of 1861 school building taken from 1895 deeds of transfer to school board	ERO	D/DO T32
P2.10	Warley Hospital, Brentwood	Ben Watkinson	
Fig 2.1	Part of Courtauld family tree	AW	

P3.1	First page of first junior log book	ERO	E / M L 194/1
P3.2	First page of first infant log book	ERO	E / M L 193/1
P3.3	Imaginary sketch of possible scene in large schoolroom with teacher, monitors, pupil teachers and pupils	D i a n a Naylor	
P3.4	Matthew Arnold's signature from junior log book 1866	ERO	E M L / M L 194/1
P3.5	Matthew Arnold's report entered in the log book by the head teacher 1866	ERO	E M L / M L 194/1
P3.6	Syllabus for infants 1878 – 9 from log book	ERO	E M L / M L 193/1
P3.7	Re-enactment of Victorian school room from 1987 pageant rehearsal	BRNTM	1994.18
P3.8	Magic lantern in Wymondham Museum, Norfolk	Tom Drury	Wikipedia Commons
P3.9	Infant building enlarged from old print 1864	BRNTM	see P1.1
P3.10	Original school building. used by infants as seen on 1895 deeds.	ERO	D/DO T32
P3.11	Tortoise stove	?	Wikipedia commons
Fig 3.1	Revised Code of Standards 1862	Curtis	p.259
Fig 3.2	Revised Code of Standards 1872	Wikipedia	2010

Appendices

P 4.1	Crittall workers on strike over efficiency measures, June 1912	BRNTM	2118
P 4.2	Lease of school by trustees to Braintree Board 1876	BRNTM	?
P 4.3	Deed of transfer of ownership 1895	ERO	D/DO/T32
P 4.4	Separate sheet attached to 1895 deed with plan showing main building and old infant school layouts	ERO	D/DO/T32
P 4.5	Plan from 1897 deed showing how lot 7 was made up	ERO	D/DO/T32
P 4.6	George Courtauld Education Charity foundation booklet cover	BRNTM	?
P 4.7	A page from the George Courtauld Education Charity foundation booklet	BRNTM	?
P 4.8 Page showing purchase of Chapel Hill Field from George Courtauld Education Charity foundation booklet		BRNTM	?
P 4.9	Infant school staff outside their new building 1897	BRNTM	3313
P 4.10	Younger children 1895-1910	BRNTM	2045
P 4.11	Class VII 1895-1910	BRNTM	3138
P 4.12	Older children 1890-1910	BRNTM	5461
P 4.13	Older children 1890-1910	BRNTM	5462
P 4.14	An infant school inspection report in log book 1890	ERO	193/1
P 4.15	Infant scheme of work from log book 1886	ERO	193/1
P 4.16	Ball frame or abacus in museum	AW	
P 4.17	Memorabilia brought in for 125th anniversary exhibition	BRNTM	1994.18
P 4.18	Children rehearsing Swedish Drill for 1987 pageant	BRNTM	1994.18
P 4.19	Foundation stone of Infant building	BRNTM	1994.18
P 4.20	Drawings of old infant building done by Mr. Clark	BRNTM	?
P 4.21	Builder's sketch of old infant school's extensions with more suggestions for creating space	BRNTM	?
P 4.22	Cover sheet of architect's specification for new infant building	BRNTM	?

P 4.23	Small room of infant building in 1981	AW	
P 4.24	Spacious hall of new infant building	BRNTM	2325
P 4.25	Funeral procession of Edward VII showing the three buildings in place	BRNTM	?
P 4.26	Older pupils with backdrop of old infant building	BRNTM	2331
P 4.27	Junior classroom in large room showing fixed hall partitioning 1981	AW	
P 4.28	Junior classroom in large room showing folding partitioning and track of removed partition 1982	BRNTM	1994/175.25
P 4.29	Marching corridor Long room made with glass partitioning 1981	BRNTM	1994.175
P 4.30	Flooring changes in museum showing positioning of old partitions	AW	
Fig 4.1	Basic plan of 1861 building & new 1911 extension, as in use 1981	AW	

P 5.1	A bird's eye view of Braintree circa 1920	BRNTM	3011
P 5.2	Mr. Baines' memorial	AW	
P 5.3	The Hicks family outside their shop in Church Street, soldiers from the Notts and Derby Regiment 1915	BRNTM	2039
P 5.4	Flyleaf of book presented to commemorate coronation 1937	BRNTM	1994.18
P 5.5	Mr. Davies' memorial	AW	
P 5.6	Staff photograph 1926	BRNTM	2389
P 5.7	Older boys 1930	BRNTM	2322
P 5.8	Older girls 1930	BRNTM	2326
P 5.9	Younger juniors 1930	BRNTM	3310
P 5.10	Infants 1928	BRNTM	3311
P 5.11	Infants 1930	BRNTM	2237
P 5.12	The Bartram honours board	AW	
P 5.13	A Bartram prize from 1956 brought in for 1987 exhibition	BRNTM	1994.18

P 5.14	Page from school magazine 1930s	BRNTM	HTL 1095
P 5.15	Exterior of school late 1930s	BRNTM	5758

P 6.1	Exterior of school early in WW2	BRNTM	537
P 6.2	Exterior of school 1981 – no railings	AW	
P 6.3	Infant log book showing air raid warning record	ERO	193/4
P 6.4	Mrs. Hilda Carver weaving purple silk velvet for the coronation of Elizabeth II at Warner Mill, in 1952	BRNTM	3373
P 6.5	Page from Centenary Booklet by Miss Jarvis	BRNTM	?
P 6.6	Friends of Manor Parents' Association Saturday morning fête	BRNTM	1994.175.53
P 6.7	Some of the readers in use in this period	BRNTM	1994.180.74
P 6.8	Gymnastics in the canteen	BRNTM	1994.178.76
P 6.9	Sports day at the Tabor Field	BRNTM	1994.178.57
P 6.10	Mural of The Lyon in Braintree Town Hall	BRNTM	2005.34.6
P 6.11	Exterior of canteen 1981	AW	
P 6.12	Interior of canteen set for lunch	BRNTM	1994.178.10
P 6.13	Kitchen of canteen in use 1985	BRNTM	1994.175.9
P 6.14	Infant classroom 1982 showing partition and lighting suspended from false ceiling	BRNTM	1994.175.26
P 6.15	Assembly hall in large room showing remains of partitioning at ceiling height, folding partition removed 1981	AW	
P 6.16	Urinal for boys, using back wall, 1981	BRNTM	1994.175.6
P.6.17	Girls' lavatory with fixed wooden seat pieces 1981	BRNTM	1994.175.8
P 6.18	Wash hand basins for use by girls and female staff 1981	BRNTM	1994.175.7
P 6.19	Portaloos in playground across the road	BRNTM	1994.175.11
P 6.20	Only internal source of hot and cold water in junior building	BRNTM	1994.175.24

P 7.1	A class in the 1911 extension in 1982	BRNTM	1994.175.21
P 7.2	A class of 28 children in one of the small infant classrooms in 1982	BRNTM	?
P 7.3	Anne's last staff photo	BRNTM	?
P 7.4	Playground mathematics	BRNTM	1994.175.51
P 7.5	Playground mathematics	BRNTM	1994.175.52
P 7.6	Braintree and Witham Times report of the entry into the NELEX competition	BRNTM	1994.181.88A
P 7.7	NELEX entry display and successful competitors 1984	BRNTM	1994.176.81
P 7.8	The infants win a NELEX award 1986	BRNTM	1994.178.66
P 7.9	A display of 4th year school journey work AW		
P 7.10	A display in the hall for open day	BRNTM	1994.177.12
P 7.11	Carpeting in the long marching corridor	AW	1994.175.16
P 7.12	Library provision in the long corridor	BRNTM	1994.177.15
P 7.13	Group working area in the long corridor with a volunteer helper	BRNTM	1994.177.18
P 7.14	Children showing off working with a computer on an open day	BRNTM	1994.177.46
P 7.15	Newspaper cuttings from the Braintree and Witham Times of the Domesday project involvement	BRNTM	1994.181.120
P 7.16	Newspaper cuttings from the Essex Braintree Chronicle of the Domesday project Involvement	BRNTM	1994.181.141
P 7.17	Children at the railway station doing their research	BRNTM	1994.176.72
P 7.18	Children walking around Stisted fields for the project	BRNTM	1994.176.60
P 7.19	Live musicians visit	BRNTM	1994.175.28
P 7.20	A performance of Joseph and his Technicoloured Dreamcoat	BRNTM	1994.176..205

P 7.21	An infant performance of Hansel and Gretel	BRNTM	1994.176.8
P 7.22	Setting off on a 4th year journey to Norfolk in 1982	BRNTM	1994.176.43
P 7.23	A boat trip in Norfolk on a school journey	BRNTM	?
P 7.24	The Friends of Manor, Parents' Association float in Braintree Carnival celebrating the 125th anniversary of the school	BRNTM	1994.180.37
P 7.25	Audrey Mullane, the school secretary for many years, in the school office in 1982	BRNTM	?
P 7.26	The school staffroom in 1981	BRNTM	1994.175.23
P 7.27	New access to junior toilets from the long corridor	BRNTM	1994.177.38
P 7.28	New roofing and doorway for girls' toilet access	AW	
P 7.29	Boys' new stainless steel urinal relocated more privately	BRNTM	1994.177
P 7.30	Braintree and Witham Times Thursday Nov 25, 1982 report on the rumours of closing the school	BRNTM	1994.181.128
P 7.31	Essex Braintree Chronicle Wednesday Nov 24th 1 9 8 2 1982 report on the rumours of closing the school	BRNTM	1994.181.128
P 7.32	The letter sent to parents about the double shift proposal	BRNTM	1994.181.128
P 7.33	Maps of proposed catchment area changes enclosed with letter	BRNTM	1994.181.128b
P 7.34	Essex Braintree Chronicle 1985 report on the possible move	BRNTM	1994.181.129
P 7.35	Braintree and Witham Times and Evening Gazette reports on the 1985 proposals	BRNTM	1994.181.127
P 7 36	Evening Gazette July 9th 1985 report of parental action	BRNTM	1994.181.130
P 7.37	Essex Chronicle report of proposed parental action Friday July 2nd 1985	BRNTM	1994.181.135
P 7.38	Essex Braintree Chronicle report on closure letter sent to parents in 1986	BRNTM	1994.181.157

P 7.39	The actual notice pinned to the wall of the infant school	BRNTM	1994.181.129
P 7.40	Braintree and Witham report Thursday March 13th, 1986	BRNTM	1994.181.173 a&b
P 7.41	Evening Gazette Wednesday April 8th 1987	BRNTM	1994.181.132
P 7.42	Essex Chronicle report on date for Closure Friday January 30th 1987	BRNTM	1994.181.111
P 7.43	125th anniversary reunion for secondary aged ex-pupils	BRNTM	1994.179.48
P 7.44	125th anniversary reunion for retired ex-pupils	BRNTM	1994.180.1
P 7.45	The Braintree and Witham Times report of the 125th anniversary meeting of four headteachers	BRNTM	1994.179.105
P 7.46	Stan Chapman, Chair of Governors at the 125th children's assembly with cake and staff lighting candles	BRNTM	1994.180.3
P 7.47	The youngest children blowing out the 125 candles	BRNTM	1994.180.24
P 7.48	Radio hams have an all-night vigil	BRNTM	1994.180.24
P 7.49	Essex Chronicle report of the 125th anniversary reunions Friday January 30 1987	BRNTM	1994.181.112
P 7.50	A pupil's thoughts in 1987 about the closure	AW	

P 8.1	Children in costume outside the Town Hall on John Ray day 1986	BRNTM	?
P 8.2	Re-Enactment of a WW2 Lesson	BRNTM	?
P 8.3	Re-Enacting a Victorian Lesson	BRNTM	?
Fig 8.1	Plan of school with Museum extensions	AW	

Index

Index

A

B

C

Index

D

E

F

G

H

Index

T

U

V

W